CRIME IN AMERICA

CURTIS DUPREE

ARCHWAY
PUBLISHING

Archway Publishing books may be ordered
through booksellers or by contacting:

Archway Publishing
1663 Liberty Drive
Bloomington, IN 47403
www.archwaypublishing.com
1 (888) 242-5904

ISBN: 978-1-4808-9308-5 (sc)
ISBN: 978-1-4808-9309-2 (e)

Library of Congress Control Number: 2020913158

Print information available on the last page.

Archway Publishing rev. date: 08/27/2020

CONTENTS

INTRODUCTION

My name is Curtis Dupree. I'm from Baltimore City; that's in Maryland. I have been dealing with the criminal justice system most of my life, from one incarnation to another. I know about life in the inner city, and I also know about the two prisons—one with bars, walls, and fences and the other without. The economic prison, that's the one robbing people of hope and destroying families. I know about a government that really doesn't understand what's going on, and what they do know, they are not willing to accept responsibility for. For example, the part they are playing in all this inner city madness, including misery and crime. What's the problem? It's not profitable to deal with the problem or even to address the problem. This would mean they would have to confront the fact many people are profiting from the problem itself. Just leaving it alone is the mindset. Why deal with it? Just lock them up and kill them. Right?

How will it ever be possible to pass legislation that can help bring about meaningful change in this country when the government is making policies coming from a place of ignorance, indifference, and greed? The government talks to the government: "What do you need to address the crime and poverty?" Ask us what we need to make our lives better, the ones that are living in poverty every day. You don't know us, and the people you are asking don't know us either!

Trump is inviting police, people from the business community, and others to the White House to discuss ways to help the country "be great again." These groups can't speak for us; they don't know us and don't care to know us. Later in this book I tell you how the policies involving business people contribute to the poverty and crime in this country. The president doesn't have a clue about what's going on in this country. At least when it comes to crime. He's talking to a bunch of old white men with old white views of the world.

We are trapped in a government-made class that has only a few ways out. Such as jobs that have us living from paycheck to paycheck, scared that if medical problems arrive or we get laid off, we might lose everything. We find some ways to supplement our incomes. That's where—by any means necessary—thinking comes in. We may even have to settle for living as homeless people! Do you know who is sleeping on the streets and under bridges? The mentally ill, people who just gave up trying and refuse to fight anymore. Also included are ex-offenders, people addicted to drugs, and husbands and wives who are so overwhelmed they have lost their jobs, homes, and children. They all found themselves living like this—stuck—and can't find a way out!

All the laws dealing with the poor have been passed to punish us for not accepting a lifetime of not having enough to support our families. The lower class, which is a government-made class of people who leave home each day with the thought, *I am going to make sure that my family has everything it needs, no matter what!* "Me. Me. Me. I don't care about anyone else; this is for my family." And beliefs like, "I will kill or die for my family."

The government has done a good job of getting us to feed

off each other. I don't really know if this was intentional or just happened. What I do know is that we have come from a time where neighbors looked out for each other and cared about each other regardless of race, religion, or sex. Now we are in a time when neighbors are afraid of each other. We have families, friends, and neighbors preying on each other. Trust is gone. You don't know who you can trust because people are hurting out there. They are robbing and killing each other for things that they feel they need or want. They are jealous and envious of each other as well.

Now we have gangs fighting over who will control all the illegal activities in our neighborhoods. Then you have the biggest gang, the police officers, robbing and killing with impunity, with the courts turning a blind eye to it.

Every day in the courts of America, defendants accept responsibility for their conduct. But change will never come as long as the government doesn't accept its responsibility in this madness.

I have been told by family and associates that police brutality and injustice toward minorities were going on long before I was born. In my lifetime I have seen it get a lot worse. During the times they talk about, the police didn't have respect for the people they swore to serve and protect. They still don't have any respect for the laws they swore to uphold and enforce.

The government wants everyone to respect law enforcement. This will never happen as long as they continue to treat minority communities with such disrespect. Respect is something that you earn. They can't make people respect them, but they can do things to make people mistrust, fear, and hate them.

I believe that the so-called War on Drugs was really a war on minority communities. In the eighties this was the catalyst for the push to strip poor people of their rights. If the government doesn't understand the people's concerns, it's easy to say that the people who are complaining are lazy and black or white trash troublemakers. They figure these people don't understand that the government is trying to help them. I do agree with the last part: We don't understand because the help that's being given is destroying our communities.

Some people speak out against black lives matter because they don't understand the movement or believe that blacks and other minorities should have a voice. They also feel that no rights should be respected. Refer to the Dred Scott Decision, March 6, 1857, at www.history.com. In that decision, the courts ruled that "No black person has any rights that a white person have to respect."

People who understand the movement know that they are not saying all lives don't matter; they just want this country to realize that black lives matter too. The black lives matter movement and other groups like them remind me of the Dr. Martin Luther King Jr. movement. With a little more flavor, these movements are voices that are screaming and shouting, "Enough is enough."

For years people in the communities have been telling government officials about how corrupt police and the criminal justice system is, but they are still not listening. Many in government don't care, understand, or even believe it. The big one they can't see how it affects their lives.

We are sick and tired of being sick and tired. We are done with all the tears being dismissed as exaggerations. Our pain is real, and we're fed up with the injustice. For those of you who don't know, poor white communities in this country are going through injustice from the police too. They don't complain; they have been brainwashed to believe that it's normal to be mistreated because they are poor. No one wants to see police hurt, no matter how much they are feared and despised. We know we need them to protect our families since they are trying to lock up all poor people. We need someone to protect the ones they don't get, our loved ones and friends. We don't even have a problem with them doing their jobs.

The 2016 presidential election should have shown the people in this country who had doubts. Whether or not racism was still alive and well, Donald Trump has brought them from the underground. They see him as a chance to put things back like it used to be. Do you remember when people of color didn't have any rights?

The 2016 election showed us racism is still alive in America. This is something that other countries have been saying about this country for years. It's the bigotry, prejudice, and hate we have for our own people because of our differences. In the Middle East we are called liars and hypocrites. We send our leaders all over the world. We send our religious books, missionaries, love, and peace, which are all about human rights. Here at home the rights of the poor are ignored every day. We are locked up or killed because we refuse to accept not having opportunities.

The rich keep getting richer. The poor are doing things to survive that they would have never dreamed of doing. Young men and young women are prostituting themselves just to have money to eat and have clothes. To obtain other necessities, they are robbing, selling drugs, committing murders, and doing just about anything to get ahead.

The government has created a class of the poor in which children are raising themselves in the streets. Children who believe that they must stand up and be the parents of the house. Their parents are on drugs, and some have just given up on life. One or both parents may even be in prison. There may not be income coming into the home or not enough income to pay the bills. In most of these cases, the children don't have any supervision, and there is no father at home. No one in the household is feeling good about themselves or their situations.

I hope that this book enlightens the reader as to what is really going on in our government. When it comes to addressing the issues of the poor in this country, I was inspired to write this book when I saw the movie *Precious*. When she was crying and saying how terrible her life was, the teacher told her to write!

ONE

POLICE

When I was serving time in a federal prison camp, I met people from all over the country. We all had the same complaint concerning the criminal justice system: it was unfair. I know the reader is probably thinking, *You are supposed to feel that the system is unfair to you.*

Please keep reading! There are a lot of white-collar inmates there. One day I was having a conversation with one of them. This inmate owned several pizza carryout restaurants and had members of his family in government. He asked me, "Why do black people hate the police so much?" I told him that the police were a gang that was just as brutal as the street gangs, and they operate with impunity. He said that he'd never heard that before. That conversation got me thinking, so I asked all the white-collar guys what they knew about the interaction of police and black people. They started telling me about how we don't have respect for the police, or someone is always trying to kill them. I told them what I knew for a fact; they also said they never heard that before.

Those conversations inspired me to write this book.

Change can't be made unless the problem is known. Police misconduct takes many forms:

- coerced false confessions
- intimidation
- false imprisonments
- false arrests
- police perjury
- witness tampering
- falsification of evidence
- police brutality
- racial profiling
- unwarranted seizures of property
- unwarranted searches
- sexual misconduct
- rapes
- robberies
- murders
- assaults
- drug dealing
- extortion

Some police officers use the poor community as a place to release their anger, hate, prejudices, and repressed inner bullies. These are the officers who cause all the confusion, hate, and mistrust. They're the ones jeopardizing the safety of their fellow officers.

Don't get me wrong; there are many officers who come to work to do their jobs. These officers are friendly. They walk through the communities saying things like, "May I help you with your bags?" and, "How are you today?" They stop and talk with kids. They encourage them to stay in school and listen to their parents. The worst of the worst criminals respects that and realizes that being a police officer is a career.

Readers, don't get mad, but these nice officers are guilty too! They are guilty because they know that their partners are terrifying the minority communities, but they don't try to stop them or report them. I think that's what's called "complicity and failure to act where one should act." As a result, people on both sides get hurt. And because no one in government is talking or listening, the problem is just getting worse.

Did you know that some police officers boast that they have the biggest gang in this country? If you know anything about gangs, you know that all gangs have some renegade members they wish they didn't have. But because they are members, the gang feels that they must stand with them, right or wrong.

Don't be misled; not all members of gangs are violent or crazy. Little did you know the public gets upset with gang violence, and gang members do too! What can they do? They have the best example of how a gang is supposed to support each other: the Republican Party.

Did you know that police departments and the police union in this country stand by the officers even when the evidence shows that the officers are wrong? They still try to get the officer out of whatever mess he or she is in. The police union has never seen a guilty officer.

Do your research! Police kill and lock up what they don't understand. Out of fear they beat and stomp with impunity. They choose what laws they like and don't follow the ones they don't like. The ones they like are the ones that coincide with their beliefs. These are the officers who might get someone killed or badly hurt.

What's all the anger about?

Black lives don't matter; the police have a license to kill us. It doesn't matter how old we are as long as we're black and not white. I'm not just talking about white officers. We have found that some black officers are just as bad. They also don't care about our lives. They view us as a threat wherever they see us. The law assumes things like we all are about to commit a crime or have committed a crime before. Every time police officers come in contact with us, they are scared to death. They fear for their safety. That's one of the reasons that they pull the weapons so quickly. We know this, and it makes us even more scared of them. We are scared when they watch us, and we watch them so we won't get hurt. We all know that they can and will kill us. We don't have a right to live because the government said so.

In a lot of cities in this country, people under the age of eighteen have taken to the streets to support themselves and their siblings because their families can't afford to support them, or they are on drugs or in prison. Instead of the police and the government trying to find a way to help these young people before they are killed or sent to prison for life, they choose to label all of them as thugs and constantly try to find ways to imprison their parents. They create ways and laws to bar these children's parents from any kind of government assistance and employment. I believe that the government can do great things for the youth in this country if it would just deal with the problems and stop killing and imprisoning our youth. Their lives do matter too.

To make matters worse, the police ride through the poorest communities every day assaulting people. They say things like, "Come here. Didn't I tell you I didn't want to see you no more today?" Then they beat, kick, and maybe even break something. The final assault is when they kick the person in the behind and then tell that embarrassed person, who also feels disrespected, to go on down the street. This whole scene is played out before a corner full of people, and it is degrading and humiliating.

The police may get a call: "Man in yellow jacket selling drugs." They pull up to a block full of people, grab the guy in the yellow jacket, pull him into an alley, and while people in the block are following to see what they are doing to him, have him pull down his pants and underwear and bend over so they can look up his butt. Then they have him lift his genitals so they can see if he is hiding any drugs. I have been one of the victims of this degrading, humiliating, and soul-tearing assault. It leaves you feeling helpless because there's nothing you can do about it. This situation doesn't just apply to black and brown youths. It happens to white teens too, the ones that the police consider poor white trash. I have seen white men and women beaten really bad by the police because they got caught buying ten dollars' worth of drugs. This type of behavior occurs every day, 365 days a year. It's not just a war on drugs, it's a war on the poor.

Many feel that the rights that middle- and upper-class Americans enjoy do not apply to us. Once confronted by an officer, they are at his or her mercy. The officer might say, "I would like permission to search your car." If one says no, the officer will search anyway, and if the person objects strongly, he or she might get hurt. When police come to search our homes, everyone knows not to ask to see the search warrant as that means an automatic beatdown. When they come to a home and beat and disrespect the parents in front of their kids, threatening to have the kids taken away, the kids can't help growing up hating them too.

In 2008 my fourteen-year-old son, Brian, was ordering cell phones from different companies and selling them for one hundred dollars. My wife and I didn't know anything about it or how he learned to do that. At first officers thought it was me because I had a criminal record. But because the other kids were hollering that it was Brian, the officer charged him. He received probation. I was told by one officer that my house had been under surveillance for thirty days. So they knew there were a lot of children in the house, and it was about stolen cell phones. So why all the guns? This is just another example of how the police see the poor. We must all be some kind of threat, even the children.

About a week later, I took my youngest son to McDonald's. There were a group of police cadets in there, and once Shykeem, then six years old, saw them, he started screaming, "Police, police, police!" He was hiding behind me, crying. That police raid traumatized my baby. The whole McDonald's went silent.

We have a right to remain silent. Try it if you want to, and you will be going to the hospital. We don't have the right to sit on our own front porches or steps. The police will ride by and say, "Go in the house." They treat grown people like they're children, so humiliating and threatening.

We don't have the right of freedom of assembly like the middle- and upper-class people do. We are herded through our communities like cows. We are not allowed to congregate. When we see the police—and I am also talking about people who aren't breaking any laws—we know to start moving. Just by living in the cities we all are seen as criminals until we show that we aren't. We shouldn't have to show them anything; it's their job to protect, serve, try to prevent crime, and arrest us when we commit a crime, not treat all lower-class people as though everyone is committing crimes. The poor communities are treated like we are not a part of the United States. It's like we are living in a military-occupied country. Every day the police violate our rights to make their jobs easier.

Police departments have been sending out officers with all kinds of character defects, hate in their hearts, trying to get rich quick, and out-and-out racists. They don't enforce the law; they make it up to suit their purposes. They lie to get a search warrant so they can go into homes that they suspect might have drugs or cash that they can steal. They lie in court and put drugs and weapons on people that they don't like for whatever reason. These are not wild accusations. This is based on facts. There have been many cases where the police department couldn't cover for officers, and they went to prison. These former officers are all over the state prison and the federal prison systems. Their convictions include murder, drug-dealing, perjury, assault, rape, sexual assault, stealing, and planting evidence.

Police officers are known for being in covert positions so they can watch criminal activities. But did you know that some of them use this position to rob the drug dealers? The officers know that there are usually twenty-five pills in a pack. At $10 each, that's $250. The officers wait until the dealer sells at least a four-pack and then drive up, jump out of the car, take the money, smack the dealer upside the head, and tell him they don't want to see him any more that day. This kind of behavior happens in every city in this country every day.

Some male officers also search females in the streets, knowing they are supposed to call for a female officer. They do this because they have no respect for us. Rapes and sexual assaults are also everyday occurrences committed by some officers. While in covert positions, these sexual predators in uniform sit in their cars, watching the drug traffic and looking for nice-looking women that they hope are on parole, probation, or have good jobs. They watch them purchase the drugs and then follow them from the drug strip. The officers then jump out and say, "We saw you buying drugs back there." She's scared to death. "Are you on parole or probation?" If the answer is no, then they ask, "Are you employed? Well does your employer know that you use drugs?" In either of these scenarios, the offer is no arrest if she is willing to have some kind of sex with them. The women usually submit because they don't want to go to jail. I have been told by many women who have experienced this that the shame and guilt never leave. They may confide in someone very close to them, but that's as far as it goes. That shame, *Maybe I shouldn't have been there. If I wasn't on drugs, this wouldn't have happened to me. It's all my fault.*

Rape and sexual assaults are reported often, but the police department dismisses them as junkies lying. Police departments read the complaints often enough, so they know who the predators really are, but they choose not to act. The justice department needs to clean house and stop turning a blind eye to the bad cops. The country needs officers whom we can trust and respect, not officers who will treat us with disrespect. I know that some of the readers are saying, "I don't know any officers like that." You don't know the officer; all you know is what he or she shows you. And all we know is what he or she shows us, which is that a lot of them need to be in handcuffs.

There are officers who have been dealt with administratively for abusing their power and disrespecting the people they swore to serve. A lot of these cases could have been criminally handled, but they chose to handle it in house. This is the criminal justice system we are told to respect. There have been many cases where officers were reprimanded for forcing confessions. A reprimand? How does that work?

Someone has been sent to prison for something that he or she didn't do, and the officer gets a reprimand. Where is the justice in that?

In 2007 I had a criminal case; I was charged with assault and robbery. One evening I went back to my old neighborhood in Baltimore, Maryland. I was standing in front of my grandparents' old house—they had moved several years earlier—talking with childhood friends. A car stopped in the intersection of Fayette and Smallwood Street, and a police car pulled up behind it. Three women jumped out of the car, one yelling, "There he is. Right there in the blue jacket." She was pointing down Smallwood Street. The police sped around them and flew down Smallwood, chasing the guy. One of the women in the car knew me. She asked, "Curtis, what are you doing around here?" I said I was born and raised around here. I asked her what was going on. She pointed to one of the women and said, "My aunt was in Turks Bar, in the packaged goods section when a guy hit her in the face and snatched twenty dollars out of her hand. I said I was sorry to hear that. She asked me if I knew the guy in the blue jacket. I said no and told her I had to go. The two women with me started walking me to my car. I was parked in the next block, on Smallwood, up from Turks Bar.

When we reached my car, the police car that was chasing the guy in the blue jacket stopped. An officer jumped out, gun in hand, and ordered, "Get on the ground." When I asked what this was about, he grabbed me, swung me on my stomach, and put the handcuffs on extra tight. By this time two more police cars pulled up. Another officer asked what was going on. The officer who had me replied, "This is the guy who assaulted and robbed the woman in the bar. Then the officer asked about the women. "Oh you can let them go," the officer holding me replied.

During all this, I was yelling that the cuffs were too tight and that he had the wrong guy. I screamed that I was just with that woman. The arresting officer dragged me and yanked me to my feet, intentionally twisting and breaking my right hand. The women who were with me hollered that I wasn't the one. They told the officers that they were going back to the corner to get the woman who was assaulted, and she would straighten this out. I was in so much pain. When the victim arrived, she said that I wasn't the man. "Well I'm locking him up anyway because he looks like him to me," the officer said.

She told the officers, "My family knows him well, and this man doesn't even have a blue jacket on. And you never saw how the man looked."

A large crowd had gathered, hollering, "Let him go." When the police van arrived, I was still screaming about my hand. I was thrown in the van and taken to a hospital, where X-rays confirmed that my hand was broken. A lieutenant came to the hospital and told the arresting officer there was a large crowd outside saying that I was arrested for nothing. "What's going on? Did the victim say it wasn't him?" the lieutenant asked.

"Yes, but I have a feeling that it is him," responded the arresting officer.

The lieutenant then asked me if I had a record. I asked him what that had to do with anything. When he asked me again, I said yes. "For what?" he asked. When I said drug-dealing, he said, "Lock his ass up."

I was taken to central booking and denied a bail. When I saw the pretrial lawyer that night, she told me that I would go before the judge in the morning. I told her about what happened to me. She said that she would check into my story, and if it were true, she would request that the judge give me a bail. I told her, "Bail? You should ask that I be released."

She just said, "We'll see."

When I went before the judge in the morning, my pretrial lawyer argued that I shouldn't be arrested. After the judge heard all the information, he released me on $5,000 bail. Thirty days later, I went to my preliminary hearing. When my case was called, the victim was at the prosecutor's table, arguing with him. The whole court could hear her saying, "I'm telling you that I know him, and he's not the man." When the judge asked what was going on, the victim said she told the officer who arrested me and the other officers, "This is not the man that assaulted and robbed me. Now I just told this man the same thing, but he is determined that he wants to offer him probation." The judge asked if this was true, the prosecutor answered yes. The judge threw the case out and told the arresting officer not to leave the courtroom.

I filed suit for an illegal arrest and assault for breaking my hand. I went to three arbitration meetings, where the officer and I had to talk. At each hearing, I broke down and cried because I was so angry and felt so humiliated. I believe that this officer saw me as less than nothing. The officer kept saying that he was sorry, but I knew he was lying. Right after this happened to me, I found out that he was one of the main officers terrorizing the neighborhoods disguised as police work. I agreed to a settlement of $15,000 because my lawyer told me that I had a good case, but because I had a criminal record, I wouldn't get much more than that if I went to trial. I was disgusted. This was criminal minds at work in the criminal justice system. People with the same criminal mindset are in charge of arresting, prosecuting, and judging people. Where is the justice in that?

In the eighties I was selling drugs. One of my sisters— CalPearl—asked me to talk to her new boyfriend. She was concerned about his safety on his job. He worked as a security guard at an all-night A&P Food Market. She told me that most nights he was fighting shoplifters. So that night I took her to the market around midnight. Just as she said, when we pulled up to the market, he was out front arguing with four guys, saying, "This is my stuff, and if you come in here again, I'm going to hurt you bad." They replied by calling him all kinds of names and threatening him.

We went into the market, and a little while later, he came in. CalPearl introduced us; his name was Tysean. I asked what that was all about. He replied, "This is my market and no one is going to take anything from me."

I asked, "Aren't you supposed to detain the person that you catch shoplifting and then call the police?"

"I'm not doing that. I'm going to beat them so bad that they won't want to come back here."

I then said, "Won't that get you fired or locked up?"

"I don't care," he answered. When he was fired about two weeks later, he came to me, looking for work. I told him that I sold drugs. He said that he knew and wanted to come on board. He had an area to sell in and just needed product. I gave him heroin and cocaine. Things were going well with him for about six months, and then I heard that a woman in Glen Burnie owed him $300. He and his crew threw a lot of the woman's furniture out in the street. I didn't like that and didn't approve of that kind of stuff. So even though I liked him, I let him go. We remained friends, but we just couldn't do business together anymore.

While all of this was going on, CalPearl got a job as a housing authority security officer. She worked in several housing projects. Now keep in mind that Tysean and she just graduated from high school. Two months after I let Tysean go, she got him a job working as a security guard too. A year later, I was arrested. I received fourteen years. During that sentence, they came to visit me often.

One day when I'd been in prison for over four years, I brought my photo album to the rec room. Some of the guys wanted to see my photos. While I was playing cards at one table, some guys from my city were at another table with the album. I was startled by loud laughter and jumping around. I turned to the table, and several of the guys were shouting, "That's him, yo." I asked what was going on, and one of them brought my album to me and asked who a guy was in one of the pictures. It was Tysean. I said that he was my brother-in-law; he and CalPearl had gotten married. They started telling me about him terrorizing most of the projects in the city. They said that he had most of the dealers afraid to come out when he was working. They said that he would beat someone—male or female—down every day he worked. They knew so many people who wanted to hurt him badly, but they didn't want that kind of heat on the projects. They told me that he made his own laws, enforced that law, and issued out punishment.

The next time Tysean and CalPearl came to visit me, I asked them about what I heard. Tysean said it was true. He said that they are supposed to be afraid of him and run when they see him coming. "If they don't leave the area, I bang all of them in the mouth." I asked him if that was something that he was taught at housing. "No, that's my law."

I asked CalPearl why she got him that job. "You know he's crazy." She started laughing and asked me if I would still trust Tysean when I got out. I said, "I will respect his job, and I won't do anything to harm our friendship."

Tysean got really upset. "How can you say that? That's not for us. I wouldn't do anything to hurt you, man." I didn't respond to that; I just let it go.

He left that day, and I didn't see him for about three years. That's when I was released from prison. The day I was released many people told me that Tysean was now a police officer and terrorizing whatever jurisdiction he was assigned to. The next day I visited him and CalPearl at their home. I didn't feel welcomed, so I never went back. Tysean is now a homicide detective. God help us.

I want readers to know that there are many Tyseans on the force in this country, "playing police." As long as they believe that they don't have to respect us, the problem this country has with the police will continue. If nothing changes, nothing changes. I believe that this book will continue to be relevant until change comes about. I encourage readers to do their own research at least every month to see if their behavior changed. Are they still being charged with crimes, murder, assaults, rapes, and robberies? Do they still disrespect the lower class? That is, if you even care. Look for anything that you believe they shouldn't be doing. The problems don't just start with the officers on the streets. The commanders tell them to ride around and arrest people for anything so they can make their quotas. Most of the arrestees are released within twenty-four hours with no charges. These include people who are going to work, doctor appointments, picking their children up from school or practice, and going to school. I have been told that the arrest is really to see if the person has any warrants and to meet the officer's quota. Please stop believing everything police say. It's been documented that these people lie too. I find it ironic that the justice department and the courts can always explain away an officer's conduct by saying he or she acted in good faith. Time and time again it has been proven that there are a lot of bad officers in our communities who are liars and thugs.

There should not be any good-faith exceptions. Laws

are made by humans, and we all have our stuff with us, our likes and dislikes, and our prejudices. So this notion that the police's word is like God's Word, unchallengeable, is a method to deliver injustice. The following are some cases I recommend that you look up. But please do your own research as well.

Three Miami police officers were arrested in drug sting. One suspect agreed to provide a uniform and badge for a planned hit.

February 6, 2018, a motorist was robbed of $25,000. The crime was not carried out by civilian criminals but by Baltimore officers.

On November 1, 2018, an ex-Philadelphia police officer pleaded guilty to drug conspiracy. Former Baltimore and Philadelphia police officers were also charged with conspiring to sell drugs.

On July 29, 2017, criminal cases were dropped after video allegedly shows officer planting drugs in Baltimore City, Maryland.

In December 2017, officers planting drugs in a suspect's wallet selectively filmed only portions of the arrest to implicate the man for drug possession.

A New York Police Department officer received a sentence of fifteen years in prison for selling stolen guns to drug dealers. He flooded the streets with illegal guns.

According to an academic report dated Sunday, October 21, 2018, a police officer in Prince George's County, Maryland, was charged with more than four hundred rapes and six hundred groping offenses.

On December 4, 2015, it was reported that a group of racial extremists within one Alabama police department planted drugs and weapons on young black men for more than ten years, leading to nearly a thousand wrongful convictions. The report stated that up to a dozen officers were members of a neo-confederate group.

On January 24, 2019, a veteran Miami cop pleaded guilty in a drug case. He recruited fellow officers into a racket that protected drug dealers and transported cocaine loads.

On January 30, 2018, detectives on a Baltimore gun trace task force committed a home invasion.

On February 13, 2018, a jury found some former Baltimore police detectives guilty for their roles in a large-scale corruption scandal.

Arapahoe County Sheriff Patrick T. Sullivan was busted for meth and sent to the jail named after him.

On October 18, 2019, police planted drugs on a homeless black woman.

Members of the New York Police Department were charged with raping a woman in a police van on October 27, 2017.

Milwaukee, Wisconsin, police officer Dominique Heaggan-Brown was charged with second-degree sexual assault on October 20, 2016. He sexually assaulted men and women.

A Tennessee police officer was charged with rape and sexual assault on October 3, 2016. The attacks occurred during traffic stops.

An Oklahoma City police officer was convicted and sentenced to 263 years for raping black women.

A Northern California police officer was arrested on twenty-two sexual assault charges and kidnapping with intent to commit rape.

I recommend you read the following articles:

filmingcops.com/planting-drugs-to-arrest-innocent-people-is-part-of-the-game-cop-admits-that-false-arrests-happen-a-regular-basis.

John Thompson, *DC Post*: One of the biggest defenses in Contraband cases is that law enforcement officers planted evidence and lied to make the arrest. Cries from defendants were largely ignored by all parties involved, including the jurors, because of psychology. You have the defendant, and you have law enforcement. People have been conditioned to rely on the word of authority as truth. The question is, Should this be the case?

thefreethoughtproject.Com   Real   life Training Day.

Cocaine-pushing cop robbed drug dealers and FBI agents while on duty. Office Brian Jones was terminated from the Jackson Police Department and charged with abusing his authority to commit extortion. The FBI began investigating Jones over a year ago, after local residents repeatedly complained about the dirty cop.

Alabama: www.Innocentproject.org/category/ news.

Deleted documents show Alabama police planted drugs and guns on innocent black men in a decade-long span. Members of a specialized narcotics team operating in Alabama were accused of planting drugs and weapons on innocent young black men in a series of wide-ranging abuse spanning nearly two decades. See also, an article in the *Henry County Report,* henrycountreport.com/blog/2015/12/01/leaked-documents-reveal-police-department-planted-drugs-on-young-black-men-for-years-district-attorney-doug-valeska-complicit.

The Associated Press, color of lawlessness; sexual abuse by police, nationwide women under siege project: http://interactives.ap./2015/betrayed-by-the-badge-/SITEID=apmobile.

Following a year-long investigation across the country, one hundred officers had lost their licenses over six years for sexual crimes, including rape, sodomy, possession of child pornography, and sexual misconduct. Abuse of women of color is an underreported story. By Johnny Silvercloud.

Wils S. Hyton, *New York Times*, September 28, 2016, www.womenundersiegeproject.org/blog/entry/the-color-of-lawlessness-abuse-by-the-police-nationwide.

Marilyn Mosby is Baltimore's top prosecutor. She took this job believing she could fix the broken justice system in the city. She's a young black woman who knows the problems, but the powers-that-be wanted to leave the broken system broken: Baltimore vs. Marilyn Mosby.

In case your memory is a little foggy, Mrs. Mosby was the prosecutor who decided to charge the officers in the Freddie Gray case. Twenty-five-year-old Gray was arrested in April 2015, and protests over his death turned to incendiary violence. Mrs. Mosby, the state's attorney, in the midst of that unrest took to the steps of the war memorial downtown to announce that she was filing criminal charges against six police officers over Gray's death.

"I have heard your calls for no justice, no peace," she announced before a bank of television cameras as she spoke about the outrage across the country. She hoped this would calm the simmering terror in the city. At least it temporarily elevated Mosby to the role of proxy for a nation reeling with outrage and disbelief over the failure of other prosecutors in other cities to indict other police officers for killing other black men, including Michael Brown in Ferguson, Missouri, and Eric Gardener in Staten Island, New York. Mosby was sued for defamation by five of the officers she indicted. She has been subjected to more or less constant assault on conservative airwaves, accused of criminal misconduct by Donald Trump, and featured on the cover of the police magazine *Frontline* under the headline, "The Wolf that Lurks." A steady barrage of racist hate mail and death threats poured into her home and office.

One night in mid-September, a cop with two decades of service on the police force spent an hour and a half venting about Mosby's intractable incompetence. In case you are picturing some old white dude with a revisionist hankering for the good old days of zero tolerance, I want you to know that this cop was a woman of color with staunchly liberal views who firmly supported mandatory police cameras in ready acknowledgment, for example, that under the mayoralty of Martin O'Malley, in 2000, Baltimore police behaved like a goon squad, rounding up black people in mass arrest without a scintilla of probable-cause. O'Malley had officers clearing corners and violating the constitutional rights of everybody.

A friend who covered the city for a major newspaper told me on more than one occasion that whatever you thought about how Mosby handled the trials, one had to admire the guts she showed taking on the police department, knowing that it would alienate many of the prosecutors in her office and every cop in the city. Even if you didn't think she did the best job prosecuting the case, many had a lot of respect for her. Mosby tried to make a difference even though the police hated her, and the prosecutors didn't like her. We need more people like Marilyn Mosby to stand up to and challenge injustice regardless of personal consequences. Now she's alienated by a system that she worked hard to be a part of. Mrs. Mosby, I say to you and people like you don't stop trying to make a difference. You are in a class of people from the past who have died to make us free to have rights and opportunities.

In Baltimore in 2017, eight city police officers were charged with racketeering, armed robbery, conspiracy, extortion, filing false police reports, and overtime fraud.

To the Baltimore City Police Department and police all over the country, you are a big part of the problem. That's why you are not respected and trusted. Now we have Donald Trump, a president who wants you to abuse people you arrest. He is so uninformed; you already abuse people you arrest. Please don't listen to him. If you don't change the relationship between you and minority populations, things will only get worse.

It amazes me that police always say that they, "Can't do it alone. We need your help in stopping crime in the communities. See something, say something." Well you see something and say something. They know who the perpetrators are in their departments; they work with them and socialize with them. They know the ones who are terrorizing our communities. They ride through our communities in search of someone to arrest, and he or she is sitting right beside them. We can't do it alone. We are living in a time when everyone is ready to pull out the cell phone and start videoing whenever the police confront someone in the community. We need the so-called law enforcers to enforce the laws that govern all of us, not pick and choose who they think the laws should apply to.

TWO

THE WAR ON DRUGS

The real war is on poor blacks, browns, and the whites who associate with us. In 1970, the heroin that was coming into this country was around 70 to 90 percent pure. Once the heroin hit the streets, that was when I started using. During that time, a person had to have been using for a long time before becoming physically addicted.

The people I started using with were still doing the same things I was doing. We kept our appearances up. We all wore nice clothes and still went out partying. We used it three or four times a day. We would get locked up and never experienced a physical withdrawal. And we did this for years. It's not like that today. Everyone in the community can see that you are on some kind of drugs. Today's heroin and crack users don't care about appearances or anything else. They live for the next fix. They live to use and use to live. Back when I was using, you hardly ever saw a woman using. Most young men started because of the rumor that when you took heroin before sex, they could have sex for hours—the Viagra and Cialis effect. The rumors were true. Back then, heroin was so strong that two or three of us could get high off one bag. Not today. And the heroin today doesn't have the Viagra or Cialis effect.

The US government did two main things to create this massive drug problem in this country. It started burning poppy fields, coca plants, and marijuana crops. These actions made the drug cartels call for early harvesting, which also diminished the drugs' potency. It also made it almost impossible for the drug cartels to obtain the chemicals needed to process the drugs.

As a result, this action only made the problem worse. The cartels make more money and more people become addicted because the crops are harvested early, and the quality of the drugs are weak. The cartels were forced to find other chemicals to use in procession. Because the quality of the drugs was so poor all over the country, users had to spend more money to get high and break more laws.

Because the drugs are so weak, the dealers in this country try to find ways to make them more potent. They throw anything they see on the internet or hear about in the streets— including Fentanyl—into it, hoping that it will work.

The chemicals they now use make people physically addicted after using once a day for two or three days straight. So it's not the drug that has the addicts going crazy. It's the chemicals the cartels are now putting in all their drugs.

The war on drugs really hurt minority women and children. The government locks up thousands of husbands and fathers. Now there is one paycheck and one parent. And sons feel they have to help their mothers. They turn into little men overnight; playtime is over. If they are at least eleven years old, they are thinking of ways to make some money to help out.

Because there's only one paycheck, and in some cases

no paycheck, things have changed. The lifestyle the family is used to is gone. In its place is a woman who is trying to hold things together, She finds that her children are getting out of control because they think they are grown men and women, maybe because they have brought a few dollars to the table. In a lot of situations like this, the one parent is mainly concerned about keeping a roof over the children's heads. We have some women who can handle their children under any kind of pressure, but it's not a lot of them. Just look at the juvenile institutions and the prisons. If there's no positive male figure involved in the children's lives, they will build their core beliefs from information that's learned in the streets—lies, untruths, half-truths, misinformation, bias, racism, stereotyping, sexism, and disrespect for other people. Oh, and a dirty mouth. The streets also teach the importance of getting money by any means necessary, regardless of what you have to do to get it. Street teachers believe this garbage because they were taught this garbage.

In this country's poorest communities, a woman often finds herself in the situation where her man is incarcerated, and her children are getting locked up or being taken from her because she can no longer take care of them with the little she has. She never thought that she would need government assistance. She now finds herself doing things for money that she couldn't imagine in her wildest dreams she would do. She's a beautiful woman, but now when you look at her, you can't imagine a time when beauty lived there. The only way she knows to deal with the pain, depression, and so much loss is through alcohol, drugs, or whatever. To support her self-medicating, she has sex with men or women or both. Before this dramatic life change, she wouldn't have given them the time of day. Her self-esteem is so low she finds herself crying and praying a lot. Neither brings her peace. She misses her

family and her old life. Now when she goes to sleep, she prays
that she won't wake up.

When I was released from a drug conviction in 1995, I
went right back to selling drugs because I knew that just like
before, I wasn't going to get hired anywhere because of my
record. I made a good amount of money. My plan was to
make enough to open a grocery store. At this time in my life,
I was so tired of prison. I worried all the time about being
arrested. It had gotten so bad, that I started having panic
attacks.

I wound up opening several stores. I stopped dealing. I
had nice cars and a house. My family, friends, and neighbors
were good. I started feeling better about myself, and the panic
attacks stopped. Then something happened. I didn't realize
that the income from the stores wasn't sustaining my lifestyle.
I was spending more money than I was making, and bills
started piling up. I started losing everything that I had built.
Everywhere I turned there was no help, and the panic attacks
started up again. The Small Business Administration told me
to close all five of my grocery stores and take a class that they
offered. I was asking for help to keep my businesses open and
being told that because I didn't have any credit, I should just
close the stores, take the class, and start over again.

The advice I received from friends, family, and associates
was to take the money I had left and buy some heroin and
cocaine, and get busy. I didn't like that idea, and I wasn't going
to get rid of my stores, even though I was closing them one
by one. I didn't want anything to do with the drug business
anymore. Prior to all this, I wasn't drugging or drinking. But
when the pressures of life started hitting me upside my head,
I got drunk almost every night. I was told by many hustlers
that I was crazy for not running back to the drug life. Some
even said that I was crazy for leaving it in the first place.

I stopped drinking and drugging on November 16, 1983. But when my depression got so bad, I started drinking and drugging again in 2014. They didn't understand I was tired of living like that. And I knew that because of my record, if I was caught, there was a chance I might die in prison. My health and age had me constantly worrying about that.

Despite all the things I'd tried, all my stores were gone. I struggled to pay the bills every month. My back was against the wall, and I went back to the drug life, but not like I left it. I only had enough money to buy two ounces of crack and fifty grams of heroin. Since there's no wait to sell, I had to send it to the streets. I started a food truck business that operated during the day. My plan was to have a few people selling the drugs for me. That plan didn't work out. Everyone I gave them to messed up the money. So I parked the truck and went on the block myself. I know you are probably thinking, *He's making one bad decision after another,* and you are right.

I didn't know that so much had changed since I was hustling on the corners back when I was fifteen years old. Now I was back at it aged fifty-nine and feeling stupid.

The question I was asked over and over again by family and friends was why I waited until my money was gone to go back to the drug game. My answer was always the same; I was trying hard to find a way not to go back to prison. It seemed like no one could understand that I was really trying to change. It was known by everyone I knew that if I said I was going to do something, they could take it to the bank. All that started to change when the pressure of life got real and then got real, real. I found myself borrowing money and not paying it back. I told my kids that I was going to do this or that and then not do anything. Not being able to keep my word was eating me up inside.

Back on the block, I only came out at night. I never came

out during the day because I was ashamed. I didn't want the other hustlers to see me. Remember I had been a big shot. But in time, the street started talking, and then everyone knew. I was so depressed about how my life had changed that I started drinking Grey Goose liquor every night I went to the block. I dealt with this being back on the block for three years, and I hated every night of it.

I wasn't really accomplishing anything. I don't care what I tried, it just didn't work. The cocaine was garbage, and I was making just enough to pay bills. My wife was so used to me making money, she started changing on me. That really hurt. But what really hurt was when I let my kids down.

Before I went back to the block, I used to go through the old neighborhood once in a while. I would stand around, talking to old neighborhood friends. Each time I came through I never noticed the level of poverty around me. So my first day on the block, I felt so overdressed. I had on the latest gear, but I was surrounded by people who had lost all hope of a better life and didn't know where their next dollar was coming from. I felt overdressed, and I think some of them thought I was showing off.

The real messed-up thing was that I knew a lot of them from childhood, but I hardly recognized any of them. That's how bad life had beaten them up. I would sit on the same steps, and most of the people who came by knew me. As time went by, women I grew up with would come up and offer sex for drugs. They would say things like, "Can you help me get my husband [son or daughter] out on bail?" Or, "Can you give me a few dollars so I can get something to eat?" Or, "You know, I always had the hots for you." And the real crazy one, "You know, my daughter just turned eighteen. Do you want to meet her?" I was sick of the mess.

After about a year of this stuff, all my workers started

calling me the social worker because every night I came out, I gave away $100 worth of drugs. My workers got mad every time I did this. "Here comes the social worker," they would say. I wasn't making the kind of money I should have, but it made me feel a little better about myself, and because for the first time in my life, I could see the effect that drugs were having on the community. I felt shame that I was playing a part in this madness.

My life had become unmanageable. I didn't know what to do. I knew I no longer wanted to be part of the madness. I didn't want to go back to prison; I wanted my life back. I found myself talking to God a lot and crying and praying. I was so unhappy.

On February 19, 2014, I was arrested. It was my worst fear, being taken from my family. I had a panic attack. The police were about to call an ambulance, but I told them that I wasn't leaving the house while they were still searching it. Once I was placed in the police car, I felt relief instead of worrying and fearing the unknown. I was tired of worrying about money, tired of the distance between me and my wife, tired of the lack of control of my life. Back in prison again, this time for six years, I believe that God heard and answered my prayers.

My story is not just mine. Ex-offenders all over this country can relate to my pain. We are tired, but with no job, no money, and no opportunities, it's almost impossible to change our lives. The war on dealers is also a war on our families and the whole community.

Who came up with this idea anyway, releasing thousands of prisoners every year back into the communities with $25— that's for states, and in the federal system it's $20—and a ticket to get us to the state where we will live? Not taking into consideration that he or she may not have any kind of support system or how long the prisoner has been incarcerated. Because of criminal records, most of these thousands won't get employed, won't receive any government assistance, and in most states, not allowed to live in government housing. We have a mayoral election coming up soon in Baltimore, Maryland. Some of the candidates are talking about taking the driver's licenses from ex-offenders once released, and when they get a job, take 3 percent of their pay.

This is what's known as the economic prison, the one with no bars and no legal way to support oneself and family. We can't contribute to society. We can only be a burden in one way or another. Poor blacks, browns, and whites in this country have goals and dreams too, and all the laws the government passes won't stop us from trying to have a better life for ourselves and our families. We want better. As you can see, we all are not going to sleep under bridges or in parks and eat in soup kitchens.

We are not going to see our children without, regardless of how many obstacles you put in our way. A lot of us sacrifice ourselves every day to give a better life to our loved ones.

This drug war has messed up our communities so much that not just the young guys take to the streets to help out the family. Young women are out there too. Now when I drive through neighborhoods, I see young women in mobs, hanging out on the corners, selling drugs, and prostituting themselves.

It amazes me how this government can be so concerned about children in other countries being hungry and sold into prostitution when the same things are going on here, and nothing is being done about it.

Most of the laws that were passed in the 1980s through 2000 were to address the drug problems in the inner cities. They didn't address the problems; what they have addressed are the symptoms of the problems, and they are doing a poor job at that. The course they chose to take is insane. Crime is still high, recidivism still booming, and prisons are still overcrowded, and children in the thousands are growing up with one parent in the home.

I can't overstate it enough. Children are not mature enough to understand that they are too young to parent. They are reacting off their feelings, that strong wanting to help feeling. So when the parents tell them not to do this or that, they don't really hear that. It's nothing like a child's love for his or her parents. They don't like to see them sad, hurting, and unhappy. Their little minds are asking, *What can I do to help?* Because of the immaturity of these children, most of their choices are bad and have dire consequences, like being killed in the streets, life in prison, or receiving the death penalty.

Recidivism

The criminal justice system reports that former inmates, on average, out of prison three years. It's a miracle that we last that long. This system is designed for the inmate to fail.

This is a big business, modern-day slavery. Prisons are the new plantations. Today we are not bought and sold, but laws are passed aimed to imprison people of color. This is not me being paranoid. It's a fact.

We are separated from our families and used to keep the prison business booming. If the inmate has some skills, he or she may be able to earn up to forty cents an hour. Plumbers, electricians, painters, roofers, carpenters, computer and equipment operators, clerks, teacher's aides, kitchen workers, laundry workers, sanitation workers, and so on can earn up to nineteen cents an hour in the federal system. States pay less.

Some prisons have contracts with private companies and use us for the labor. At least thirty-seven states have legalized the contracting of prison labor by private corporations that have operations inside the prison. These include Pierre Cardin, Macy's, Northern Telecom, Intel, Texas Instruments, Compaq, Honeywell, IBM, Motorola, TWA, Microsoft, AT&T Wireless, Target, Dell, Hewlett Packard, Victoria's Secret, and Revlon. These companies, and others like them, make billions off this endless supply of cheap labor. We have to work, and we have to accept the pay or be placed in lock up.

This is what's called "American greed," and there are no incentives to change anything. Greed and corruption laws are constantly being passed to put us in prison longer. Mandatory minimum and maximum sentences don't rehabilitate and don't stop the crime in the country. Why would a businessperson want to stop getting rich? They don't have to pay benefits or overtime. Do you remember how slaves were treated?

Congress is complicit in this thirst for cheap labor. It passed laws that set automatic minimums and maximum sentence lengths, guaranteeing lengthy prison terms and thus, greater profits for companies in the prison business.

The prison wants all the money an inmate earns in the institution, including money an inmate may receive from family and friends. But keep in mind most inmates do not receive money from the outside. Inmates are responsible for paying court fees, $25 every ninety days. Once released, the inmate must pay delinquent child support or be sent back to prison. Inmates buy personal items from the commissary, the institution store, that sells mostly dollar store-type merchandise but charge top dollar for it. Phone calls are

$3.15 for fifteen minutes; sending and receiving e-mails are five cents a minute. There are many sites that allow the public to download music for free, but we have to pay $1.55 for each song. It costs fifteen cents a page to print legal and personal papers. Copies are fifteen cents each. Inmates have a $2.00 copay to see the doctor or nurse. Most of the time, regardless of what an inmate's complaint is, he or she is told to purchase over-the-counter medication from the commissary. In some federal institutions, inmates have to pay to wash and dry their clothes.

Once an inmate is released, the parole and probation departments start demanding money. We must pay, and I don't think they really care where the money comes from. If we can't pay, as I mentioned earlier, that's grounds to be sent back to prison.

It's clear to me the lack of employment opportunities and denial of any government assistance—including housing, food stamps, educational grants, and loans—and the stacking of child support payments, court fines, and fees for parole or probation costs. It ensures that most inmates won't be able to save any money for his or her release. Further ensuring that inmates will likely have problems within their first months of freedom.

Some states have programs like a one-stop career center. They help ex-offenders with employment, educational grants, child support issues, and so on. I applaud these kinds of programs. They do good work, but they can't do it by themselves. These programs have long waiting lists for services. And once you are in the program, they require you to take certain classes. So it will be a while before the ex-offenders' immediate needs are addressed. In the meantime, some are homeless, hungry, and have no money. Some even have immediate psychological issues that need to be addressed.

Not all inmates have a support system, family, and friends. Once released, there's no one there to help them with the transition back into society.

Readers may think that I am paranoid, but during my research for this book, the dots are connecting. There is no incentive to stop crime. People like President Trump and his friends are getting richer and richer from this country's mass incarceration. It is more of an incentive to continue mass incarceration than to pass legislation addressing poor people's issues.

Mass incarceration has not had a real effect on lowering crime rates. What we have here is greed under the guise of protecting the country. Mass incarceration and detaining of immigrant nonwhites is the criminal justice system at its worst. Poor people are being rounded up like runaway slaves to work in prisons all over the country, but we are led to believe that the criminal justice system is mainly going after major drug dealers, rapists, and murderers. They are really just going after bodies. It doesn't matter if the crime is something minor, the prison is always looking for bodies.

In many states, employment depends on the prison industry. No prisoners means unemployment for many. There are so many businesses making a lot of money off of mass incarceration. Bail bondsmen have always made a lot of money off of the poor, but now, that business has made them filthy rich. Don't forget the lawyers. A mother will spend her rent money to hire a lawyer to try to free her child.

The judge gives a person with no income a $100,000 bail. Now family members don't want to see the person in jail, so they have to get $10,000 in cash (10 percent) for the bail bondsmen. There's nothing like a mother's love. She will go without before she sees her child in prison.

Have you noticed that most prisons are located in predominantly rural areas near large white populations? Many correctional officers are carrying on a family tradition. Generation after generation of their families have worked there. What would happen if the prisons closed?

It amazes me how the judicial system will find ways to fine or lock up a poor person because of trash in the yard and say, "Look how they live." It may be like that because you don't care about the neighborhood either. No jail, no fines. Local governments allow property owners to neglect and abandon their properties. it seems to me like governments— local, state, and federal—are always trying to find ways to make the poor pay more. They are allowed to rent dilapidated houses to the poor that can't afford to pay more. They are allowed to depreciate the value of the neighborhood with their raggedy houses. The tenants are not to blame. The tenants are not responsible for the outside of the property. We have whole blocks boarded up all over the country. Please stop lying about the poor.

The Border Wall, Trump, and Motives

I believe Trump's border wall is not for the reasons he campaigned on. One thing about living the lifestyle I have lived is that I know a crook when I see one. It's hard to pull the wool over another hustler's eyes. This president is not concerned about stopping the drug epidemic in this country. He just wants to stop the cartels from making all the money. Most drug users in this country are addicted to pharmaceutical drugs, including fentanyl. The president wants to clear the way for his big pharmaceutical company friends to take over the drug market so he can get his cut.

I read that he constantly complained that other rich people wouldn't accept him as one of them. I guess they could see that he was a dressed-up trash can filled with money. That's just one part of it. The man is racist to the core.

There was a time when the drug suppliers had to go through crime families to get drugs into our communities. Now they go around them. The president and his millionaire friends can't compete with the influx of drugs coming in from all over the world, meaning they are not getting any of that money. Just listen to how he talks. President Trump sounds like a crime boss.

Trump and his associates are not the kind of people who care one iota about poor people or the drug epidemic. They don't care if businesses are poisoning our waters. They don't even care if their tax dollars would help the economy. They just think that low-income people should pay while they find ways not to pay their fair share. For Trump and his friends, if it doesn't make money, it doesn't make sense.

Trump told the world that he is greedy. He and his associates probably have money invested in prison stocks. Check out those members of Congress too who fight so hard to keep things the same. If I am right, why would the opponents of prison reform mess with their bottom line. I believe there needs to be an investigation into all the people who constantly vote against prison reform, including their family investments. Just like Tom Price, former secretary of human and health services. He was voting on legislation concerning the pharmaceutical companies while making money from having stocks in the companies. So how does that work? we need to keep an eye on all the people who act like laws don't apply to them.

How long will we allow our public officials to constantly use good faith as an excuse for basically every wrong thing they do? When we see government officials eventually charged or convicted of wrongdoing, that shows that there shouldn't be a good faith exception. The good faith exception should have no place near policies or decisions that affect people's lives.

Should their words be automatically taken as true? I don't think so. Just about every day somewhere in this country, a public official is caught lying, stealing, or is involved in some kind of corruption. Facts, not exceptions to facts. We have people in this country who have lost their lives, liberties, and property because of the so-called good faith exception. Facts and only facts should be the only standard in making binding decisions. We can't continue to believe, "He [she] is a good person, so I believe he [she] is not lying." We must always remember that it is a human behind those words that are automatically taken as truth. When someone speaks on any topic, the individual is coming from a place of self-interest and core beliefs.

President Trump has been given the good faith exception by his followers. They believe basically everything he says. He declared a new war on drugs but has proposed cutting the money that's needed to help people get off drugs. He continues to push Congress to pass a health-care bill that would really hurt his supporters and millions of other people in this country. With this bill, the only ones to benefit are the insurance companies. He said that if the bill passes it will get better down the road. This is coming from a president who is constantly caught lying. He promised to make America great again, but what are we willing to give up for this great promise? People are being asked to support evil, selling themselves for what they think would be a better life. But what about the millions of Americans who would be hurt by his plans of greatness? As long as I can remember, I've heard stories and seen movies about how Satan promised to make lives better by using lies.

I am a man who has lived his life trying to achieve the American dream. I will admit that I made a lot of bad decisions and have done wrong, but with all my faults, I'm still a loving and caring person. I care about the poor, elderly, hungry, homeless, sick, and the drug addicts and alcoholics who are still suffering. And I care about the injustice that black and brown people have to deal with every day. Why don't you care? You should because life is full of ups and downs, and you don't know when or if you, your friends, or family members will be among the millions who will be hurt under Trump's great again plan. One day you may need the services that you are so willing to give to Satan.

Now let me tell you about the three kinds of ex-felons. The first is the one who has the support of family and friends or knows someone who knows someone who can help with employment. That's the one who stays out of prison. The second one has stopped trying to get his or her life together. This one has given up on life. This is also the one who says, "I'm not going back to prison no matter what." And most don't. They don't have jobs or any means of support. They can't provide for their families, so they leave home depressed, hurt, mad with the world, homeless, and on drugs or alcohol or both. This is the only way they know to make it through the pain each day.

The third one is the one who says, "I'm not going to be homeless no matter what." I am in this group. I don't believe anyone has the right to tell me that I can't support myself and my family. This is the United States of America after all.

My children look at me with respect because they know

that I love them and will put myself in harm's way to make sure that they have a good life. They saw the war that I was having with myself. I would tell them that I hated selling drugs and that I hated the part I was playing in the madness. But I had to continue doing things that I hated to support my family. How is it that I had to make choices like that in this country?

Some readers may be wondering, *Who takes care of them when you are in prison?* The point is that when I am there, I'm there. I am not going to leave my family and go live in a park. I love being a parent. I love knowing that they know they can count on me. I try to show them and tell them that I love them and care about their futures. I feel good about myself today. But I don't believe that I would feel this way if I would accept being homeless, with my children seeing me with no place to live and beaten down by life, hurt, and shame. I don't believe I could deal with that. If I had to choose between my children losing respect for me or prison, I would choose prison any day.

I have two daughters who are licensed practical nurses (LPNs), Shameke and Shanny. I have two daughters who are child-care specialists, Shaniqua and Shamir. My son Brian is a phlebotomist. Another daughter, Simone, works in civil service and social work. I also have a younger son, Shykeem. He's seventeen years old, and when he really needed guidance, I wasn't there. He is now having run-ins with police. Worrying about him and feeling that I let him down is killing me. When I was in court in 2015, he told the judge that I tell him all the time that I don't want him to be like me or any of my brothers, that I want him to be better.

To meet me is to like me; the judges, prosecutors, probation officers, pretrial officers, teachers, neighbors, all the children in my neighborhood, and prison personnel like me. I am known wherever I am for helping people. But if you read my rap sheet, you would probably say, "That man doesn't belong in society."

These are especially old charges, stuff that took place when I was between eighteen and twenty-one years old. I am now sixty-five years old and still being denied the right to be a productive citizen and to reenter society as a free American with rights and opportunities like the rest of America.

I believe that Congress, courts, police, and the companies that benefit from mass incarceration should be charged with conspiracy for their parts in creating a system of recidivism for people of color and other minorities. This needs to be investigated.

Families who have lost loved ones to the streets are torn between physical and psychological pain. The love that they have for you, in most cases will come in last every time when it comes to their drugs. They hurt you, steal from you, and lie to you constantly. When they hurt you, it's not intentional. The pain and psychological trauma leaves no room to be concerned about whether they are hurting you. I am describing the life of an addict.

They steal from you because it's convenient and because they believe you won't call the police. Most don't really want to hurt anyone, but things happen when the body is saying, "Fix me." Talk to any addicts, and they would tell you to stop the pain they would do just about anything. One thing I notice is that the professionals who speak about drug addiction never talk about what an addict goes through once he or she gets high. After all the lying, cheating, and stealing to get high, you will find most addicts going off to themselves, enjoying the high. But that is also the time when reality sets in. "What have I done to my life?" The addict feels guilt, shame, and regret. This is when addicts think about the choices they made. They may cry and pray. They think about and regret stealing from their loved ones because they know that their loved ones are always worrying about them. They feel shame for letting their kids down and feel angry with themselves for being so weak. But once the high is gone, the cycle starts all over again. Some have broken the cycle by themselves, but most need a lot of help. They have a disease that can be arrested with help. I want the families and friends to know that their loved ones are struggling to get back to you. They love you and want to change. You can't imagine the pain that an addict is going through knowing that he or she is hurting people who care about them. I know it's hard, but please don't give up on them.

My step-grandfather, James, had a son named Butch who served in the Vietnam War. He was a highly decorated medic. When he came home from the war, he was also a full-fledged heroin user, like so many who came home from that war. He was living with his mother, Irene, when he got sick. I still don't really know what his ailment was, but he was bedridden. Irene was a nurse, so she took care of him. He slept in a hospital bed in the dining room. My brothers, his friends, and I stopped by often. Irene had someone go and buy him heroin every day. A mother's love.

When James heard about this, he was really upset, even though he never really had any dealings with Butch. When he asked, "What kind of mother would buy dope for their child?" I tried to explain to him that his son was dying. He was still calling him a "dope head" and his mother "stupid." When Butch died, he had a beautiful military funeral. I was sitting beside James, and while the preacher was telling us about the things Butch did in the war and how many lives he saved, James kept whispering to me, "Why are they making all this fuss over this drug addict?" I told him that Butch wasn't always a drug addict, and he was still his son.

We don't need more drug wars. We need to address the plight of the poor in this country. When you have families who are unsure if they will have something to eat tonight, it is hard for people with good intentions to help the poor when these families are overwhelmed and constantly worrying about immediate basic needs. If your help doesn't include what they need right now, you are basically wasting your time. If what you have to say is not helping the problem right now, it's probably not that helpful. Religious institutions and mentors that are trying to give the youth a moral compass are competing with the street teachers. The latter are teaching them how to take money home every day to help their families today, not in the distant future. And when they do listen to you, they are just being polite. That's real talk.

Open your eyes and ears, and try to provide programs that will provide real economic opportunities for the poor. We don't need more of the same.

THREE

THE COURTS

In most criminal cases, the courts view the overall procedures in the light most favorable to the government, the same government that is not there to seek justice but for career promotions. Prosecutors are known for hiding evidence favorable to the defendant. They encourage witnesses to lie and threaten innocent people with long sentences, even life in prison, in order to get them to plead guilty to crimes that they didn't commit.

When a person pleads guilty, the judge will ask, "Are you pleading guilty because you are guilty? Have you been threatened or promised anything?" People who have never been in this situation can't imagine the fear the person has about answering this question. If the person makes the wrong decision, he or she may lose his or her life or liberty. But by telling the judge the truth, defendants are afraid that the government may get mad and withdraw the plea offer. For example, instead of five years, the prosecutor recommends a severe punishment, which the court usually goes along with. Because of this, defendants remain silent. There's no justice in this system. The courts allow the prosecutor to make plea offers that include the defendant saying on the record that he or she won't ask for an appeal. So if years later a defendant finds evidence that may lead to exoneration, he or she can't do anything about it. That's not justice; that's the prosecutor wanting a conviction no matter what. The court, as a whole, is just as bad in most cases. There is a time limit on filing appeals. If late, the defendant is out of luck. That's not justice; that's injustice. Injustice must be challenged wherever and whenever it's found. If a person has been sentenced to forty years and after serving twenty-five years discovers evidence to show that the trial wasn't fair or proof of innocence, how can it be right for the courts to say it is too late for justice.

The country is split. There are laws for people of means, and then there's laws for the poor. For example, a person that has money doesn't need money but can steal millions of dollars and cheat on their taxes and rip off their employers and the taxpayers. They also pollute the water and air for profit. Then they get off with probation, a fine, or a light sentence. A poor person who steals under $1,000 is probably going to prison for years. So we have the one who just wants more money being shown love over the one who needs the money.

When appeals courts make decisions about whether to hand down a favorable decision on inmates' appeal cases, they consider how many inmates their decision may affect. Appeals courts don't want to help too many inmates. That's why so many of the US Supreme Court decisions aren't retroactive. Where is the justice in this practice? Wrong is wrong, no matter when it happens.

How can it be justice to make life-changing decisions, taking into consideration how many people the decision will affect. How can it be justice to rule in one case that an inmate's rights were violated, yet in a similar case, the decision doesn't apply because the appeal was late. If black, brown, and poor white people can't look to the courts for justice, then where should they look?

I find that the courts are more concerned about technicalities than justice. "I told you that you had three days to file. You are two days late." This kind of thinking has allowed many people to stay in prison that should have been set free. I believe injustice should be challenged and exposed anywhere and anytime it's found, regardless of technicalities.

Once a person is sentenced to prison, he or she is trying to find a way to regain freedom. We use what resources the institution has in its legal library. Please keep in mind that we are lay people in the law. Some have never seen a law book. Some are trying without counsel to prove that they are innocent. Others are saying that they didn't receive a fair trial. The courts use our ignorance of the law and its technicalities to keep us in prison. Laypeople are being held to the same standards as lawyers. How can the courts not see that something is wrong with this?

Once in prison, an inmate has to hope and pray that a white person is challenging the same issue on appeal so that he or she can reap the same benefits of a favorable decision. Normally inmates' challenges are ignored. Most of the issues that are raised are viewed as unimportant or frivolous. And even if the inmate does receive a favorable decision from the court, the prosecutor's office will fight tooth and nail to try to convince the court that the favorable decision shouldn't apply to this inmate.

The courts continue to give the police leeway to deprive poor people of basically all the rights guaranteed by the US Constitution. The courts allow the justice department to invade the poor communities in order to find any reason, legal or illegal, to arrest all black and brown people, so we will be in prison or under some kind of government supervision.

I can walk into any supermarket in any black neighborhood, and most or all the people in there have someone in their immediate families in prison or on probation or some other kind of supervision. There's something wrong with this picture.

The courts treat black and brown children like their lives don't matter. They have no problem sending a young first offender to prison for a minor offense. In most cases, they will be assigned to a medium-security prison. No young, white. a middle- or upper-class first offender will be found in any medium-security prison for a minor offense because the criminal justice system takes into consideration their age.

The same courts that send our children to prison regardless of their age may send them to prisons housing violent sexual predators. These prisons are for serious offenders, not for nonviolent first offenders. This unjust system has thousands of our young serving time with hardcore prisoners. What are they doing there? We are shown in so many ways that our lives don't matter.

Our government has played a major role in destroying many families because it doesn't understand the problems of the poor and how crime relates to those problems. The government rushes to pass laws that they feel will address the problem immediately, not taking into consideration how those decisions and laws will be enforced, the impact on the communities, and whether the interpretation of the law or decisions will be enforced fairly.

Congress is another gang that shows street gangs how they should be loyal to their members, no matter what. The GOP is willing to destroy this country for its members. It's not America first; it's their gang and a white people first agenda.

When Barack Obama became president, the GOP openly said it wasn't going to work with him. Based on what? The man hadn't even taken office yet. So what was the problem? I can say it: It was because he was black. They hated that a race that once was slaves in this country now had one of its own as president. On the day that he took office, some of them said all kinds of nasty things and just being disrespectful. These are the same ones who can't see anything wrong with Trump. But if Obama did any of the things this white man is doing, they would be trying to burn down the White House

I recommend you read these cases. But do your own research, and stop listening to the lies.

> Walter v. United States (7 cir. 827 F.3d 682, 2016 BL 211140). Vehicle stop. Questioning begins after issuance of warning. The motion to suppress cocaine found during a traffic stop was denied; officers have a grace period to ask investigatory questions following the completion of a traffic stop, provided that it does not impose an inconvenience. How in the world can the court know whether Walter was inconvenienced? Walter is the only one who knows that. After Walter received a traffic ticket, he was detained for another thirty-six minutes. I know that some are thinking, *Walter had cocaine*, but how did the officer know that he had cocaine? The overreach of the police and the courts condoning of this behavior are unjust and inexcusable. In the

court's view, police can do no wrong, but if they do, it wasn't intentional.

You are on your way to work, to the hospital, to pick up the kids from school, or some other kind of emergency. Would you find it acceptable to be detained for thirty-six minutes after the officer has given you a ticket for a traffic violation. "Can I search your car?" What is that all about. Our courts seem to have no problem with it if the person is black or brown or a poor white person. Do your research, and you will find that this is true.

United States v. Gomez, 2017 BL 433602, 2d cir., No. 16-181-cr, 12/5/17. Traffic stop bad, but evidence is still good. The US Second Circuit Court of Appeals ruled that drug evidence recovered during a traffic stop is still admissible in court even though the stop violated the Fourth Amendment. The stop is illegal under the US Supreme Court 2015 decision in Rodriguez v. United States. But the good faith exception to the exclusionary rule applies because the stop occurred before the Rodriguez decision. So officers reasonably relied on precedent that allowed the stop at the time. Here we go again. If the Supreme Court found that kind of stop was illegal in the Rodriguez case, then it should be illegal regardless of when it occurred. Why couldn't the officer have known it was illegal and did it anyway? Oh, I almost forgot—good faith exception. They don't lie.

United States v. Johnson, 7 cir. No. 15-1366, argued 11/30/16, on rehearing in 823 F.3d 408. Several judges on the seventh circuit seemed receptive at oral arguments on November 30, 2016, to the suggestion that a special street crime unit in Milwaukee violated car passengers' right when they used a suspected parking infraction as a pretext to pounce on the vehicle in SWAT team fashion in the hope of discovering bigger and better things. There is much dislike of the police, and you can understand why when they overreach like this, Judge Richard Posner said at the en banc hearing. It sounds like the government wants us to adopt the rule that gives police authority to go down rows of parked cars in our major cities and demand that all passengers get out whenever it appears a car has overstayed its welcome at the parking meter, said Chief Judge Diane P. Wood.

California Bar Embraces New Ethics Rule expanding prosecutor's duty to disclose, Lance J. Rogers in Washington at LRogers@bna.com.

California prosecutors may soon be called on to take a more active role in preventing and even rectifying wrongful convictions under new professional conduct rules that were approved October 1 by the state bar's board of trustees. The rule would make it clear that prosecutors have an ethical duty to disclose any evidence or information favorable to defense without regard to the anticipated impact of the evidence on a trial's outcome. The new rule would also obligate prosecutors to take action when they learn of evidence indicating that a person convicted of a crime didn't commit it.

This is what's going on in our courts. We have to have rules to make them administer unprejudiced impartial justice for all. That's sad. I cannot stress it enough; evidence and facts should be the only things that matter and that the courts rely on when considering whether what an officer meant to do was unfair, unjust, and not law. The court is not in a position to say with any certainty what the officer intended to do or not do. Facts, and facts alone, should always rule in any and all courts. Stop relying on the good faith exception to deny people their lives and liberties.

Kentucky Bar Ass'n v. Thornsbury, 2017 BL 91479, Ky., No. 2016-sc-000607-BK, 3/23/17.

West Virginia Circuit Judge Michael Thornsbury pleaded guilty in 2013 to a felony involving charges that he instructed a police officer to plant drugs on his secretary's husband and later arranged to have the man arrested on a bogus larceny charge after the drug scheme fell through. He was disbarred.

King v. Hardwood 2017 BL 95527, 6th cir. No. 16-5949, 3/27/17. Immunity for grand jury testimony will not apply to police who falsify affidavits or fabricate evidence to seek a baseless conviction.

In an attempt to solve a cold case murder, an officer voted an affidavit purposefully leaving out evidence proving defendant Susan Jean King did not commit the murder. This included the fact that she had one leg and couldn't have on her own dragged the victim's 187 pound body to her car and then dump the body in the river.

Hartley v. Sanchez 10th cir., 810 F.3d 750, 2016 BL 6261, 84 U.S.L.W. 947, 98 cl 337. Defendants are not entitled to qualified immunity in this civil rights action stemming from the elicitation of the confession to burglary and sexual assault from the plaintiff, who has substantial cognitive disabilities. The plaintiff claims that the defendant committed malicious prosecution in violation of the fourth amendment by using a false confession to institute the legal process and cause continued pretrial detention. The plaintiff has provided factual allegations and details that would plausibly indicate that the defendant either knew his confession was untrue or acted with reckless disregard of the truth.

Neal v. Kubsch, 7th cir., 838 F.3d 845, 2016 BL 314248. The habeas corpus petitioner is entitled to relief.

The state court rendered a decision contrary to, or an unreasonable application of the US Supreme Court's decision in Chamber v. Mississippi, 410 U.S. 284 (1973). It excluded at the petitioner's capital murder trial evidence that was easily the strongest evidence of his innocence.

Alisa Johnson (ajohnson@bloomberglaw.com), Brand v. Casal, 2017 BL 453206, 11th cir., No. 16-10256, 12-19-17. Police aren't immune from civil liability for refusing to allow a Georgia woman to cover her exposed breast during her arrest.

On December 19, 2017, The US Court of Appeals for the eleventh circuit held that transporting Tamara Brand to jail with a breast exposed and the use of a taser on her when she was trying to dial 911 were distinct constitutional violations of the court.

In the court's opinion, given by Judge Beverly B. Martin, a reasonable officer would have known that subjecting Miss Brand to the indignity of exposing herself to countless strangers for an extended period of time for no legitimate law enforcement purpose would violate her Fourth Amendment right to bodily privacy.

For those who don't know, this practice is played out in almost every poor community. It's nothing for a child to see a man's or woman's body parts exposed when being arrested.

Bernie Pazanowski (bpazanowski@bloomberg law.com).

A police officer is immune from a suit claiming he violated the Fourth Amendment by killing a fleeing suspect, the US Court of Appeals for the Sixth Circuit said December 27. Officer Lowell Phillips acted objectively unreasonable when he shot Laszlo Latits at the end of a car chase in 2010 the court said in opinion by Judge Jane B. Stranch.

Nevertheless, Phillips is immune from the suit because no controlling authority was clearly established at the time that Latits's constitutional rights were violated, the court said.

I say that the law is clear. He was unarmed and running away from the officer. That's murder. Decisions like this are what make the police feel safe in committing all kinds of illegal acts and disrespecting the people that they are supposed to serve.

Jessica DaSilva (jdasilva@bna.com), Cleveland v. Bradshaw, US, no. 16A226. SCOTUS. The court denies application from defendants claiming actual innocence, September 21, 2016.

If you know anything about the Innocence Project, you know that they must believe you are innocent to take your case. In this case, the defendant is serving life in prison for a 1991 murder. The decision to deny the appeal was not based on whether the defendant's issues had any merits because the US Court of Appeals for the Sixth Circuit concluded that no juror could find the defendant guilty based on that new evidence. The denial was based on the fact that he did not file his appeal in a timely manner.

Here we go again, playing the technicality game. The courts consistently find that technicalities rule over fairness in justice.

Jessica DaSilva (jdasilva@bna.com), Asay v. State, 2016 BL 428654, Fla., No. Sc 16223, 12-22-16 and Mosley v. State, 2016 BL 248542, Fla., No. Sc14-436, 12-22-16. Two December 22 death penalty cases from the Florida Supreme Court have effectively specified a cutoff date for challenges under US Supreme Court decisions overturning the above two cases. Those decisions could wind up clogging Florida's appellate court systems,

according to Robert Dunham of the Executive
Death Penalty Information Center. According
to Dunham, at the time, Florida boasted about
four hundred prisoners on death row. The
decision will call about two hundred of those
sentences into question, which Dunham said
would result in huge financial and emotional
toll on the state.

Florida doesn't have enough prosecutors,
defense attorneys, or judges to hear these
new capital sentencing hearings and, at the
same time, continue the daily operations of
the courts. You're looking at millions and
millions of dollars that will have to be spent.
Dunham said the majority of capital sentences
are imposed in an unconstitutional manner,
claiming that in the Florida cases, all four
hundred death sentences were imposed in
violation of the US Constitution because the
original death penalty statute did not comply
with due process.

Dunham said the death penalty trials were
equally unfair before Ring v. Arizona (536
U.S. 584, U.S., No. 01-488, 6-24-02) was
decided. Now the arbitrary date of when a
death row prisoners lawyer finished their
appeal determines whether they live or die.

History has shown that this is unfair and
unconstitutional. If this decision was the law
of the land, those people who were recently

found innocent of the charges that they were sentenced for would not be free today.

In Hurst v. Florida (2016 BL 7258,No. 14-7505, 1/12/16), the US Supreme Court overturned Florida's sentencing scheme because it violated the court's binding precedent in Ring v. Arizona, holding that death sentences imposed by non unanimous juries or via judicial override violated the US Constitution. Both options were available under Florida's death penalty laws.

The December 22 cases delineate the retroactivity of the ruling, finding that only defendants who received capital punishment after the 2002 decision in Ring may challenge their sentences. Mark James Asay's sentence was imposed before 2002, so his claim was denied. But John Franklin Mosley's claim was granted because the sentence was imposed after 2002.

The courts have a rush to kill. Appeals are to ensure that a person had a fair and impartial trial, and to ensure that no innocent person is denied life or liberty. I just don't understand how many people the court's decision will affect, and when the wrong was discovered have to do with justice? To find that Asay's sentence was too late for justice and the fact he raised the same issues Mosley did, is really one case of many that shows just how much injustice flows from the courts.

Lance J. Rogers (lroger@bna.com), Smith v. Alabama, U.S. No. 16-7070, stay denied 12/8/16. Alabama put a convicted murderer to death on December 8, just hours after the US Supreme Court twice blocked the procedure and then twice cleared the way for the execution to proceed.

The unusual flurry of the eleventh-hour petitions and deliberation suggest that the court remains deeply and evenly divided on the question of capital punishment. The court's four Democratic appointees—justices Ruth Bader Ginsburg, Steven G. Breyer, Sania Sotomayor, and Elena Kagan—all voted to extend the temporary stay of execution granted to Ronald B. Smith but apparently couldn't persuade a so-called courtesy fifth vote from any of their colleagues that would have postponed the execution until the court reviewed the merits of his petition.

Another rush to kill. The Supreme Court didn't even want to hear Smith's petition, and it didn't want to know if there were any merits to it. I can't see how the courts can ensure that a person was not denied life or liberty without due process and a fair and impartial trial if they won't even consider the issues in the petition.

Jordan S. Rubin (jrubin@mloomberglaw.com),
Wessinger v. Vannoy, U.S., No. 17-6844,
review denied 3/5/18.

Justice Sonia Sotomayor decried death
penalty lawyers' blatant shortcomings in
her colleagues' refusal to correct them in the
March 5 dissent from denial of review. She
did so without the company of other frequent
death penalty critics Justice Stephen G. Breyer
and Justice Ruth Bader Ginsburg.

Todd Wessinger has a major neurocognitive
disorder and a family history of poverty,
alcoholism, and domestic violence, Sotomayor
said. But Wessinger's trial lawyer never tried to
find any of this out, so the jury that sentenced
him to death never knew about it either, she
said. His state post conviction lawyers failed
in this respect as well, she said.

A federal district court granted Wessinger's
habeas petition based on these lawyers'
failures. But the US Court of Appeals for the
fifth circuit reversed. They ruled Wessinger's
postconviction counsel wasn't ineffective,
so he couldn't raise an ineffective assistance
of trial counsel claim in federal court. The
fifth circuit's conclusion, "is clearly wrong,"
Sotomayor said in her dissent.

That lower court, "found that the failure to
conduct any mitigation research was not a

result of deficient performance but a product of the state post-conviction court's denial or funding for a mitigation investigation," Sotomayor said. But the Supreme Court, "repeatedly has held that the failure to perform mitigation investigations constitute deficient performance." She continued, "The justices refusal to take up the case belies the bedrock principle in our justice system that a defendant has a right to effective assistance of trial counsel and undermines the protection this court has recognized are necessary to protect that right.

"Wessinger will now remain on death row without a jury ever considering the significant medication evidence that is now apparent. The result is contrary to precedent and deeply unjust and unfair," she concluded.

Well I don't have too much to say about this case. Justice Sotomayor basically covered it all in explaining just how unjust and unfair the courts can be.

For those who don't know, a defendant with a major cognitive disorder can be put to death in this country. Most people who have had dealings with the criminal justice system know that the prosecutor will try to have a person killed whether mentally ill or not. Justice Sotomayor is right; Wessinger will remain on death row. The Supreme Court has decided his fate. Where is the justice we are supposed to recognize and respect? All I have seen since my eyes have been opened is a bunch of people mainly concerned about their self-interests—bigots, racists, greedy, lacking morals, race-haters, liars, sexual harassers, sexual predators, bullies, and criminals who haven't been caught yet.

I am not coming from a place of hate. I'm just telling it like it is. Can you handle the truth?

Jordan S. Rubin (jrubin@bloomberlaw.com), Bunch v. United States, 2018 BL 29840, 7th cir. 16-3775, 1/30/18.

A woman wrongfully convicted of killing her son and locked up for nearly two decades continued her suit against the government. On January 30, 2018, the US Court of Appeals for the seventh circuit held that too many issues were unresolved to have granted summary judgment, the appeals court said in the ruling by Chief Judge Diane P. Wood.

Kristine Bunch was convicted of murdering her son. False testimony and evidence of a federal forensic chemist help put her away. She served seventeen years of a sixty-year sentence before the fabrication came to light. Her conviction was reversed, and she sued the government under the Federal Tort Claims Act. The district court held that the government was immune from the suit and granted summary judgment. The seventh circuit ruled the burden was on the government to show immunity applied.

Miss Bunce served seventeen years for a conviction based on false testimony and evidence. Can you imagine what she was going through? She couldn't get anyone to believe she didn't do it. Shouldn't someone be held responsible? Shouldn't she be compensated for all the pain and suffering she went through? What if it happened to you? Justice is supposed to be blind, but I know that a lot of judges are peeping under that blindfold. Some of their decisions are biased, racist, and hateful.

Alisa Johnson (ajohnson@bloomberglaw.com), Smith v. United States, 2018 BL 78536, D.C. 15-CF-677, 3/8/18. A criminal defendant had no right to cross-examine a police officer about whether the officer was untruthful in an unrelated case, the District of Columbia Court of Appeals held March 8.

Sean Smith failed to present facts to the trial court supporting a well-reasoned suspicion that Officer Damien Williams lied about having probable cause to arrest in the other case, the court ruled in an opinion by Judge John M. Ferren.

The alleged evidence of corruption inconsistencies between Williams's statements and those of the other people is too fuzzy to suggest more than confusion about the events leading up to the arrest of a man who talked with Williams and wound up with both a broken jaw and an assault on a police officer charge the court said.

Smith claimed on appeal of his firearms charge that he was denied his right to cross-examine a prosecution witness. He wanted to show that Williams was in the habit of cooking a probable cause to arrest. The court affirmed Smith's conviction, but Judge Roy Mcleese dissented.

Mcleese said Smith should have been allowed to question Williams about the unrelated arrest when inconsistencies surrounding it went to the heart of whether he was guilty of assault on a police officer or was the victim of an unjustified use of force by a key witness against him.

I find that the judicial system will protect the police regardless of the facts. When a defendant is brought before the court, he or she is hoping to receive justice, but in most cases, justice isn't there. Just look at how many criminal convictions are overturned, how many death sentences have been overturned, and how many life sentences have been vacated. That's a lot each year. Why, because some appeals judges can see by the opinions that come out of their circuit that judgments are in favor of the government too often.

The defense has the right to cross-examine any government witness, especially if there's a question of whether the witness is known to lie. The district court was wrong in denying Smith relief as Williams's character was in question. Was he the type of police officer who abused his authority, and was he known to lie? Those are questions that Johnson should have been allowed to ask.

Bernie Pazanowski (bpazanowski@bloomberg law.com), United States v. Rivera-Eperto, 2018 BL 65158, 1st cir., No. 13-2017, 2/27/18. A mandatory life sentence of a player in a drug sting will stand after the full US Court of Appeals for the Federal Circuit on February 27, 2018, refused to hear the defendant's challenge.

Concurring with the denial of review, however, Judge David J. Barron said, "The defendant argues that his mandatory 161-year sentence violated the Eighth Amendment because it was grossly disproportionate to his crime."

Nevertheless, Barron said, "I am not permitted to conclude the sentence is unconstitutional." He encouraged the US Supreme Court to revisit the controlling precedent. Five judges joined Barron's opinion, and one other filed a separate concurrence.

Wendell Rivera-Eperto didn't have a criminal record but was caught up in a drug sting. His sentence was increased by a mandatory 130 years because he possessed the gun during the sting. In Solem v. Helm, the Supreme Court ruled that to decide whether a sentence is unconstitutional, courts should look at the gravity of the offense, sentences imposed on other defendants in the jurisdiction, and sentences imposed for the same crime in other jurisdictions.

"If Solem controlled, Rivera-Eperto's sentence would be unconstitutional," Barron said. But a plurality opinion in Hermelin v. Michigan upheld imposing mandatory life without parole sentences for drug offenses, and that's what controls here, Barron said. The Supreme Court should revisit that decision.

We have five justices agreeing that the Rivera-Eperto sentence should be unconstitutional, but they couldn't do anything about the wrong that they saw. I disagree. I understand that Harmelin v. Michigan allows courts to give out life without parole for drug offenses. I don't think that's in dispute. The problem that I see is that the first circuit didn't take into account that Solem v. Helm stated that the court, in deciding whether a sentence is unconstitutional, should look at the gravity of the offense and sentences imposed on other defendants in that jurisdiction and for the same crime in other jurisdictions.

For Rivera-Eperto to have received a 161-year sentence, the court couldn't have taken its guidance from Solem. That's what makes Solem's sentence unconstitutional.

Hermelin v. Michigan does give the court authority to give life without parole for drugs, but it doesn't erase Solem v. Helms's requirements.

Jordan S Rubin (*Lead Reports,* vol. 103, 6; jrubin@bloomberglaw.com). Prosecutors Ex-DOJ officials back convicts at high court.

Current and former prosecutors—yes prosecutors—have prevailed in a pair of US Supreme Court filings against perceived injustices perpetrated by law enforcement. Their *amici* (or friends of the court) briefs lament wrongful confessions in which evidence is withheld read more like the stuff of defense attorneys and likeminded advocacy groups.

But the prosecutors and ex-officials hope their law and order credentials increase the chances that the Supreme Court hears the cases of two defendants with similar stories, Brendan Dassey and Corey Williams. Both were intellectually challenged juveniles who confessed to murders in the face of contradictory evidence. They'll both die in prison unless the Supreme Court intervenes. Outside help affects the court's decision to take or reject. The case remains to be heard, but one of the current prosecutors on the Dassey case says, "it's their duty to fight for justice and the ethical responsibility of a prosecutor is to seek justice for all the victims and the defense too!" Carol A. Simon, head prosecutor for Ingham County in Lansing, Michigan, told *Bloomberg Law* if the high court grants review, the case can be heard during the Supreme Court's next term, beginning in October.

Helping a murderer, Dassey was a subject of the 2015 hit Netflix documentary series, *Making a Murderer.* It took a critical view of the prosecution of Dassey and his uncle, Steven Avery. The prosecutors' filing signed by more than sixty prosecutors, noted that millions of Americans watched the video of Dassey's interrogation in the award-winning documentary, which prompted a public outcry over obvious failure of the system. The justices should take Dassey's case to restore the public's confidence in the justice system.

Please read this case.

FOUR

MR. AND MS. RACIST, LET ME HELP YOU IDENTIFY YOURSELF

I have found that it's not really the young people who keep the racial divide alive. If left alone, they would get along. They are wearing the same kinds of clothes, dancing to the same music, hanging out at the same places, dating and getting married. It's their parents and family members who are longing for the old days and infesting the young with the racial views. They don't like this, and they don't like that about people of color and poor white folks. If you sat down and talked with them, you would find that they believed all the problems in life happen because of people of color. Make America great again.

I believe that every school in the world should have mandatory mythbuster classes covering a wide range of topics, but mostly the topics that influence the way we see and treat each other. Even with this class, we may still dislike things about each other, but it won't be based on ignorance, race, half-truths, lies, and a lack of information. It will be based on facts.

I had a white cell buddy who was twenty-two years old. He told me that where he lived, Upstate New York, there were very few African Americans. He told me that when rode through the black community with his grandfather, his grandfather would say things like, "Look at the black porch monkeys." This happened in 2012, in line with keeping the racial divide alive.

Do you see those young white people participating in protests with blacks and shouting :Black lives matter"? They have done their homework. They researched your lies, and they know that what you have been telling them was based on your own prejudice and hate for people who don't look like you. But out of respect for you, they just let you talk and preach your hate. I am not just talking about whites when I say this. I am referring to all races that push their hate, lies, and bigotry to young people. Let those young people live, and stop trying to live your lives through them.

If you lead off with hate, then all that follows are negativity and mistrust. Your hate and prejudice will not let you see any good in another person or allow you to believe someone else could have ideas that may help the country. Hate blinds you from seeing the good and admirable qualities in another person (Philippians 4:8).

This kind of hate and misinformation passed to young people from their parents, relatives, and friends created hate and distrust for people who have never done anything to them. Information that has a flavor of bigotry, prejudice, hate, and more, and based on lies and half-truths, is passed from generation to generation. This information becomes part of their belief systems, in which it is shown in how they deal with people who don't look or talk like they do.

Donald Trump's plan to address inner city crime problems is to give the police more power to kill and arrest all people of color. And if you think that it doesn't apply to you because you haven't done anything wrong, well think again. The prisons in this country are running over with people of color who didn't do anything wrong. So black people, stop embarrassing yourself by speaking up for a president that the whole world knows is a bigot and a racist. They are his words that you keep trying to make excuses for, and his actions say, "I don't like you, and I don't want you here." When Hitler imprisoned and murdered the Jews, he saved the rich ones with the nice houses for last. But they all had to go too.

Many people don't understand just how important their words are. Words are so powerful that one word can change a life or destroy the lives of millions of people. In Germany some years ago, one man used words to manipulate a whole country of some of the most intelligent people in the world. He—Hitler—led them into a world war with just the power of his words of violence. He activated people's fears with the word, and like a big explosion, there was killing. He convinced others to commit the most atrocious acts of the time. All over the world, humans destroyed other humans because they were afraid of each other. Hitler's words, based on fear, generated beliefs that will be remembered for centuries (Miguel Angel Ruiz, MD, *The Four Agreement*, 1952).

The president and former US Attorney General Jeff Sessions want to take mass incarceration to a whole other level. What an idea! Get rid of the Latinos and all the others who aren't white. Or keep the others in some kind of servitude position. If you can see where this is going, you don't want to see the country returned to slavery and the Holocaust.

Ethnic cleansing is defined as the attempt to get rid of

through deportation, displacement, or even mass killings of members of an unwanted ethnic group in order to establish an ethnically homogeneous geographic area.

Now are you a racist?

Racism is when a privileged group uses their power to oppress a disadvantaged group. Here in America, white people are the privileged group.

If you didn't see anything wrong with white people holding signs that said, "Go back to Africa," at the White House on the day Obama took office, you are a racist.

If you didn't see anything wrong with West Virginia giving 41 percent of the vote in the 2012 primary election to Keith Russell Judd, a white supremacist serving 210 months in prison, you are racist.

If you think some races are better or worse than others, that some races are superior and others inferior, you are racist.

If you think all members of a race have certain qualities, you are racist.

Do you treat all races the same or talk to them the same? If not, you are racist.

If you don't see anything wrong with the fact that hundreds of white people go into the drug-selling neighborhoods every day, and some two and three times a day to purchase drugs to use and sell, but they are not in prison—and in most cases, when they are stopped, they are beaten up and sent home, you are racist. Prisons are for blacks and browns only

What it's like to be black in the criminal justice system, this is a system that's stacked against black American's. Black Americans are more likely to have their car searched. Black Americans are more likely to be arrested for drug use, despite the fact according to Federal data that whites use drugs at comparable rates and sell drugs at comparable or even higher rates. Black Americans are more likely to be jailed while awaiting trial. Black Americans are more likely to be offered a plea deal that includes prison time. Black Americans may be excluded from juries because of their race. Black Americans are likely to serve longer sentences than white Americans for the same offense. Black Americans are more likely to be disenfranchised because of a felony conviction. Black Americans are more likely to have their probation revoked. (WWW.slate.com August 9, 2015; Andrew Kahn is *Slate*'s assistant interactive editor. Follow him and Chris Kirk on Twitter. Chris is a web developer.)

> Almost half of the criminal law cases chosen by the US Supreme Court Justice System includes an issue of racial tension in the criminal justice system. The case lineup may indicate the Court's willingness to examine the racial impact of its procedure rules related to criminal law, a professor told Bloomberg BNA. [read the report] Lead Reports. {vol. 99, No. 24} page 718-719. Retrieved from Federal Bureau of prison premium legal library. The Court's 8 criminal law cases deal with race, but Jocelyn Simonson a professor at Brooklyn law school said it can't be considered a major Trend towards addressing issues of race unless the court start looking for racial disparities and the impacts on its own accord. The cases on the court docket deal with egregious examples of racial discrimination or biased, said Lisa Freeland, a federal public defender in Pittsburgh. The three cases that feature a racial Focus are Buck vs. Davis, Pena-Rodriguez vs Colorado and Manuel vs. City

of Joliet. While Freeland said all three cases focused on relatively easy procedure issues they all present opportunity to discuss race in the criminal justice system. Question presented in Buck vs. Davis deals with a procedure matter that would determine whether an appeals court should reconsider a death penalty sentence that was partially based on testimony from an expert who considered the defendants future dangerously higher because he was black. (Buck v. Davis, U.S., No. 15-8049, cert. granted 6/6/16. In the Buck vs. Davis case) The state elicited that testimony on cross examination and reiterated the finding during its closing. (Race Playing Larger Role in Criminal Cases at SCOTUS, Jessica Dasilve, September 28, 2016)

Pena-Rodriguez v. Colorado examines whether to create an exception to the secret deliberation policy when jurors make comments about the defendant's guilt based on race or ethnicity (Pena-Rodriguez v. Colorado, U.S. No. 15-606., cert. granted 4/4/16).

Finally, Manuel v. City of Joliet is technically about resolving a circuit split about whether defenders can file malicious prosecution claims after police falsify charges against them (Manuel v. City of Joliet, U.S., No 14-9496, cert. granted 1/15/16). The US Court of Appeals for the seventh circuit is the only circuit that doesn't allow filing claims under these circumstances. Yet underneath, the procedural issue in this case deals with officers who pulled over a black defendant, called him racial epithets, and lied about a bottle of vitamins in his car testing positive for ecstasy.

Read these cases.

Lead Reports, vol. 99, no. 24. Supreme Court. Race playing a larger role in criminal cases at SCOTUS.

16-847 Lynch v. Binderup. Firearm crime, Second Amendment-18U.S.C. 922(g). (1)-Firearms disqualifications, Ruling below (3d cir. 836 F.3d 336, 2016 BL 291173): the judgments of the district court finding that 18 U.S.C. 922(g)(1), which prohibits the possession of firearms by any person convicted of a crime punishable by imprisonment for a term exceeding one year is unconstitutional as applied to defendants who can distinguish their circumstances from the class felons historically barred from having firearms; "Black and brown" are affirmed. In this applied challenge, the challengers showed that their convictions weren't serious, and the government didn't show that applying section 922(g)(1) to them furthered its interests in keeping felons from possessing guns. Questions, are all petitioners entitled to relief from the long-standing federal statute prohibiting felons from possessing firearms, 18 U.S.C. 922(g)(1)? The court ruled that the criminal offense and other particular circumstances don't warrant a firearms disqualification. Petition for *certiorari* filed 1/5/17, by Heath Gershengorn, Benjamin C. Mizer, Michael R. Dreeben, Brian H. Fletcher, Mark B. Stern, Michael S. Raab and Patrick G. Nemeroff, all of the Department of Justice, Washington.

For those who don't know, a felon can't be in the same building with a gun. "If I visit a friend's house for the first time, and while there, the police come to the house for his son, search the house, and find a gun in one of the bedrooms. Now they are asking for everyone's ID. Remember, I don't live there and don't know what's in there. The ID is checked, and I would be arrested for being a felon in possession of a firearm" (18 U.S.C. 922 {g}{1}).

While writing this book, I let a friend read parts of it. He asked me, "Who are the powers that be that you're writing about, and what would be their motive to deny people of color a chance to succeed in this country?" My answer was anyone who holds a position of influence that can influence change. Today it's the Republican Party, the Trump administration, their followers, the racist and biased media, and the so-called religious leaders who can quote the Holy Scriptures but their lives are so far from its teachings.

Most of these people claim to be members of the Lincoln's party. They are not, so don't be fooled. They would do and say anything to portray people of color as freeloaders, dangerous, and a bunch of criminals gone crazy.

Their motive is to convince America that we are people who don't deserve any rights, none that a white person should respect. These are the people who want to make America great again. They feel that they have a duty to their ancestors to bring back the old days by any means necessary and to stay in charge.

Some blacks believe that because Lincoln's party freed the slaves and the Democrat Party is supporting black issues today, that it's safe to start dismantling the progress that the civil rights movement achieved. You are wrong. The party of Lincoln has been infiltrated by a party of "We want our families' slaves back."

Do you really believe that they gave up? Racism is real in this country; just look at the 2008 election. The day President Obama took office, there were all kinds of signs saying, "Go back to Africa," and all kinds of hateful remarks. We also had our boot-licking blacks asking, "Boss, what is that nigger doing in the White House?"

The race haters are the ones who wish to divide the country and believe that all the problems of the world are caused by everyone except white people. Now we have an administration that is pushing a racist hate agenda. I believe that the supporters of Donald Trump who deny they are racists either don't know what being a racist is or are just living in denial. Trump is the definition of a racist, and they are too. They don't care that he's a racist and a bigot. They don't care that experts say that all his plans will ruin the country. They accept the words and promises of a man who doesn't read over the people educated in these matters. Their children probably know more about what's going on in the world than Donald Trump. They are willing to take a chance on him if there is a chance that he can get the country back like it was prior to civil rights, "great again" prejudice. Misinformation, hate, and ignorance allowed them to vote for Donald Trump. The Nazis, KKK, and all the other hate groups support him because he appeals to their prejudices.

Some of Trump's followers really believe they are not like members of those hate groups. If you support the same bigotry, racism, prejudiced thinking, you are. If you believe that people who don't look like you and poor people shouldn't be here and shouldn't have any rights, you are. If you don't believe that Obamacare is good and fair for the country, and that it was designed to address the main issues concerning health care in this country, you are.

FIVE

OBAMACARE/AFFORDABLE CARE ACT (ACA) COVERAGE

Under the Affordable Care Act (ACA), perhaps better known as Obamacare, the following are some of the provisions.

- Young adults can stay on their parents' plans until age twenty-six.
- Insurance companies cannot deny coverage or charge more based on health status.
- Insurance companies cannot drop you when you are sick or if you make an honest mistake on your application.
- Gender discrimination is prevented.
- Insurance companies cannot impose unjustified rate hikes.
- Lifetime and annual dollar limits are eliminated.
- You have the right to react rapidly and appeal insurance company decisions.

- Medicaid expansion makes it available to millions in states that chose to participate in the program.
- Tax breaks are provided to small businesses that offer health insurance to their employees.
- Large businesses are required to ensure employees.
- All insurance is required to cover people with preexisting conditions.
- CHIP is easier for kids to get.
- Medicare for seniors is improved.
- All plans cover minimum benefits, like limits on cost sharing and ten essential benefits, including free preventive care, OB-GYN services with no referrals, free birth control, and coverage for emergency room visits out of network.
- Large employers must offer coverage to full-time workers by 2015/2016.
- All major medical insurance is a guaranteed issue, meaning you can't be denied coverage for any reason.
- The 80/20 rule and rate review provisions help to keep insurers honest and keep rates down.
- Hospitalizations are covered.
- Laboratory services are covered.
- Emergency services are covered.
- Maternity care is covered.
- Mental health and substance abuse treatment are covered.
- Outpatient ambulatory care is covered.
- Pediatric care is covered.
- Prescription drugs are covered.
- Preventive care is covered.
- Rehabilitative and rehabilitative services are provided to help maintain daily functioning.
- Vision and dental care for children are provided.

In 2012 I was doing quite well financially. Whatever my family needed, I could provide. We didn't worry about medical, food, shelter, or any bills.

One day I was over at a friend's house. While waiting in his living room, I noticed his two sons and his wife were in the kitchen. One son was holding the refrigerator door, and the other one was holding his mother around the waist from behind. While watching them, I tried to figure out what was going on.

The refrigerator door slammed shut. She was hollering. Her son had just slammed the refrigerator door, pulling out a tooth. When my friend came downstairs, I told him what I just witnessed. He told me that was the third tooth she had pulled like that. He said that he even had a few pulled like that. I asked him why they did not go to the dentist. My friend said that would cost more than $100 a tooth. "Who has that kind of money?" he asked. Unbelievable.

The next day I told some people about what I saw, but not who it was. Their responses were almost universal "Where have you been? A lot of people do that." I couldn't understand how this could be going on in this country in this day and time.

I started investigating this. I found that medical coverage paid by the government for people with no income or low income does not pay for extractions and dentures. A person who doesn't have the money have to pull it himself or herself, or get up at 5:00 a.m. to get in one of the free dental clinic lines, which only takes the first eight people and only on certain days. Even the free clinics don't give out dentures. And if someone goes to the emergency room, the individual might receive penicillin and some kind of pain pill, but they won't pull the tooth. So now we have a bunch of raggedy-mouth people with low self-esteem. Now I understand why you see so many people without teeth.

I have found that state insurance is like having no insurance at all. You have a card, and you have a primary doctor. When the doctor says you need certain medicine, certain tests, or an operation, in most cases, insurance won't pay for it. But Obamacare says that if the doctor said that you need this or that, the insurance companies have to cover it.

Now we have Donald Trump looking out for the insurance companies and their rich lobbyists, trying to get rid of Obamacare so that the insurance companies can continue taking money for no real services. The Obama administration said that if insurance companies wanted to continue taking taxpayers' and consumers' money, they had to cover all services. So if you have a problem with Obamacare, it's because the Republicans who had their minds made up that no matter what Obama wanted to do, they were going to get in the way, even if it meant destroying the country. Hate is a powerful thing.

The haters don't even want to consider fixing what's wrong with Obamacare. I am not running for any office, so I can say it: They didn't want to fix it because Obama is black, and they feel that a black man shouldn't be president and definitely not a successful one. Not in this country.

News organizations were in Trump country asking people what they didn't like about Obamacare. Most responses were they just didn't like that Obamacare "mess." Then they were asked what kind of insurance they had, and most said the Affordable Care Act. When asked about how they felt about the insurance, most answered along the lines of, "Oh, that's real good insurance." So what's the real problem with Obamacare? The name Obama is connected to a black man. That's so sad. Wake up, people, because the Republican members of Congress are in the insurance companies' pockets. They have conspired with insurance companies to make sure Obamacare fails.

Trump has been trying to destroy both Medicare and Medicaid, which millions of Americans depend on. It amazes me how his supporters can believe that this man, who is rich and has a history of treating the poor like dirt on his shoes, can understand their needs and be willing to use his power to make their lives better. And this is the same man who constantly lies.

Obamacare also helps pay for our loved ones in nursing homes and for school lunches. We don't know what life may bring our way tomorrow, but some of us are not willing to stop services that we may one day need ourselves.

Obama started releasing people who were oversentenced and stopped prosecutors from overcharging defendants. He demanded fair sentencing for defendants regardless of race. Now we have Trump trying to dismantle everything Obama did and trying to outdo him. That's the deep-rooted racism in him. He's not going to let a black man outdo him. Trump signed a bill to allow federal inmates to earn extra time off their sentences. I see that as a great thing he did. But please, black, brown, and poor white folks, don't be fooled. This was not done out of compassion or concern for the inmates or their families. Those are qualities I don't believe he has.

Trump's policies are laced with malice. One has to look beyond the act. Figure out the motive, and you will see him for what he is, criminally minded. I can hear Jared Kushner and others trying to persuade him to do the right thing by allowing the inmates to receive time off their sentences: "Donald, if you do this, it will get you the votes of millions of black, brown, and poor people."

Obama pushed to have police brutality investigated and

punished everywhere in this country. Trump feels that it's all right for police to abuse their power.

Obama encouraged the business community to employ ex-offenders. He realized that no jobs meant more crime. The business community can't see the connection between crime and unemployment, or they don't care. Of all the companies in the country, only eighteen made the pledge to hire ex-offenders at the White House. That says a lot about business contributing to crime. Trump reassured the business community that he would change all that Obama mess.

Trump has threatened martial law in the inner cities to allow police to use military equipment. He's planning to oppress the poor and scare the children so badly that they might be traumatized for the rest of their lives.

A must read is "30 Warning Signs that You Are Dealing with Someone Evil", available on AwesomeJelly.com.

If you don't think this is a description of Trump, then you are lying to yourself. Love is blind, and hate is blind. Those feelings will only let you see the good in a person. But for those who are not wrapped up in those feelings, they can see clearly.

If you don't believe in what the Statue of Liberty stands for, you are among the ones who don't belong here.

The New Colossus

The Statue of Liberty

Nothing like the Brazen giant of Greek Fame with conquering limbs astride from land to land ; here at our sea-washed Sunset Gates shall stand a Mighty woman with a torch, whose flame is the imprisoned lightning, and her name mother of Exile. From her

beacon – hand glows world-wide welcome; her mild
eyes command the air-bridged harbor that Twin Cities
frame "keep ancient land, your poor, your huddled
masses yearning to breathe free, the wretched refuse of
your teeming shore. Send those homeless The Tempest
test to me. I lift my lamp beside the golden door!
                                                    —Emma Lazarus

Now under President Trump, we are building walls to
keep out the poor and oppressed under the guise of keeping
criminals out of the United States. If the founding fathers
believed that immigration to this country should have been
handled this way, the only people who would be here are the
descendants of the first Pilgrims and Native Americans. And
then, the doors would have been closed.

Trump's immigration agenda is nothing but an attempt
at ethnic cleansing. He wants to rid the country of all people
of color. Those that he can't legally deport, he plans to
incarcerate and disenfranchise.

His domestic policies come from a place of racism, hatred,
and Hitler. If you are not white, you don't belong here. The
KKK and all the other hate groups are right to think that they
have a president of like mind.

Trump wants to isolate us from the rest of the world, so
Russia, China, and North Korea can be the leaders of the
world. Why? In my research into dictators, I believe that
Donald Trump is using pages from Russia's, China's, and
North Korea's playbooks on how to be a dictator. Don't
believe all this, "I'm tough on all the dictators." It is just
an act and red meat for his base. Russia, China, and North
Korea are not paying this president any mind. And when he
had those secret meetings with Putin and Kim, I think he was
talking about opening businesses in their countries. I think

everyone forgot that during the 2016 campaign, he said that he thought every country should have nuclear weapons.

Trump's campaign for 2020 is to continue dividing the country.

Step 1: Run a campaign based on dividing the country, sowing fear, dislike, distrust, and hate for each other. Remember during the last campaign, he said he alone could fix what's wrong in this country. He is the chosen one.

Step 2: Keep telling the country that all news is fake and just believe in him.

Step 3: Give the military and law enforcement all the money they want, so they will be loyal to him and not the Constitution.

Step 4: Demand loyalty from his party members, and demand that they vote the way he wants them to. If they don't, he will threaten to go against them at election time.

Step 5: Stack all courts with judges who will side with him on any issue.

Step 6: Trump supporters have elected the first American president striving to be a dictator. Checkmate.

Even though we no longer have J. Edgar Hoover, former FBI director, to protect the country from enemies of the state, we do have the House of Representatives, who's doing its best to fight Russian operatives.

I find that I can say one good thing about Trump supporters: They are loyal. "I don't care what he does." "That's good, Donald. We love you, Donald." Trump said that he could shoot someone on Fifth Avenue, and his supporters would still support him. Was he really talking about law-abiding citizen or a bunch of crazy cult followers?

Trump promised, "I will drain the swamp and replace the swamp with the right people." "We love you, we love you, Donald."

He promised to fix Medicare and Medicaid, the problems with government waste, the problems at the EPA, and to stop other countries from cheating us in trade. He also promised to rid the country of aliens.

Now let's take a real look at what he's done to make America great again.

He constantly pushes his race and divisive agenda. Obama left office with a high approval rating, and he passed off to Trump a country coming back from a financial crisis. When Trump took office, he couldn't find anything that Obama did right. Every policy Obama had in place he changed or tried to change. He attacked the black man, not necessarily the policies.

He also takes full credit for the growth of the economy. He hadn't been in office two years when his supporters were hailing what a great job he's done with the economy. That should be unbelievable. Is he the second coming? That's Obama's economy. He got the country on the right track, and we are still moving. But let Trump and his supporters tell it, Obama had nothing to do with it. It takes a lot of hate to willingly claim another person's achievements.

Trump gives his father full credit for teaching him everything he knows. This is the same father who was arrested at a KKK rally. I wonder, *Did he also teach him to hate people who don't look like him?*

He frequently makes statements that can be interpreted as telling hate groups that their time has come. He said of a black protester to his base at a rally, "You know what we would have done to him back in the day."

Well, I can remember a time when Trump and all his supporters would have been rounded up and locked up for supporting a person who loves dictators. All around the world Trump praises US enemies. I might be wrong, but it seems to me like the White House is the Russian embassy. There are so many people working there with Russian connections, and several Russians have visited the White House under Trump.

Trump's administration and supporters would all have been charged with conspiring with Russia to overthrow the government of the United States of America if J. Edgar Hoover was still around.

Trump has no respect for the Constitution and no use for this country's rules of government. He wants to make his own rules. He seems to want a repeat of the Holocaust in real time. Immigrants are not being marched to the gas chamber yet, but they are being forced out of the country. And those who try to enter illegally, they may be killed or incarcerated. We are now living in a time when the world stands by and watches parents being deported and children left behind. We hear immigrants being called everything but a child of God. We hear hateful talk on TV, radios, in the streets, and from the White House. The world remains silent to what's happening in the so-called land of the free. Many people here have no problem with the treatment of immigrants because they have been led to believe the garbage coming from Trump and the race haters as facts. Trump and his supporters don't care about the plight of other races. They believe immigrants are the cause of all of our problems. "It's their fault that there is so much crime in this country," "It's the blacks and the Mexicans who are the problem," "The reason I don't have a job is because those people are trying to take over the country." To those who believe this garbage, I say if you do your research, you will find that every dictator used this same language. It is designed to make us dislike, distrust, fear, and hate each other.

There has been nothing but confusion:

> Trump has ordered mass roundups of Mexicans all over the country.

> He has shown a real love for dictators.

> He said that he wants to make America great again, and he thinks that he is doing just that.

> He spreads hate and lies everywhere.

> He's trying to take health care from the poor.

> He's telling the police that it's all right to use brutality and violate people's rights. For years people in this country have been screaming about police brutality. Now we have police on video beating and killing us—especially blacks and browns—and the government still won't act. The police always say that they fear for their life. We hear this often, so this is supposed to give the police a license to kill us. To that I say, if they are so scared of us, they need to get a different job.

He has allowed his administration, his family, and himself to rob taxpayers with this tax cut and some of his other policies.

He's being investigated for all kinds of criminal behaviors, but no one should be surprised. He told the whole world that he's greedy.

Obama put a stop to big businesses polluting and poisoning our waters. Obama joined the rest of the world in fighting climate change. In Trump's mind, if it doesn't make money, it doesn't make sense. There is no such thing as climate change. To stop pollution, he described, if it's not making money, then there's nothing wrong with a little contamination in the water. That's the mindset of our president.

The GOP (Grand Old Party—Republican Party)

Republicans are willing to stand by and watch Trump divide the country and try to isolate us from the rest of the world. They have no problem with him sucking up to enemies of this country. They allow him to send our men and women to war because he doesn't like Obama's policies concerning Iran; he prefers us to have two countries at once to worry about nuclear weapons. Let me get this right. He constantly tries to turn our allies against us, and at the same time start a trade war and a fight with two countries that have nuclear weapons, North Korea and Iran. All while plotting to take Iranian oil. That man is a genius?

So that they can pass some legislation they know Trump

will sign, Republicans are willing to let him cause mass confusion. Have we ever had so many protests on so many issues back-to-back? The Republican Party is more concerned about what they and their donors want. Instead of doing the work that they were sent to Congress to do, Republicans try to give this president, with all his character flaws, a win, no matter how many people will suffer under his policies. They have closed their minds to any kind of morals, honesty, and decency. What we have here is a Trump Congress, not the country's Congress.

I don't know about you, but this man reminds me of Adolf Hitler (World Book H-9 2005 Edition). Hitler was a skillful politician and organizer. He became a leader of the Nazis and quickly built up party membership through his ability to stir a crowd with his speeches. Hitler attacked the government and declared that the Nazi party could restore the economy, ensure work for all, and lead Germany to greatness again. Hitler also wrote that Germans represented a superior form of humanity. They must stay pure, he said, by avoiding marriage to Jews and slaves. Hitler blamed the Jews for all the evils of the world. He accused them of corrupting everything of ethical and national value. He claimed that "By defending myself against the Jews, I am doing the Lord's work."

Most German people and the leading politicians did not want Hitler to become chancellor. They knew that he would make himself dictator and set up a reign of terror. Germany's president, eighty-five-year-old Paul Van Hindenburg, had serious misgivings about Hitler, but he was persuaded by his friend and his son Oskar to accept Hitler's promise to act lawfully if he were named to form a government. So on January 30, 1933, Hindenburg named Hitler chancellor. To me, this sounds like the Republican Party members trying to decide whether Trump can be trusted with the country.

There were only two Nazis in the cabinet besides Hitler, Hermann Goering and Wilhelm Frick. The rest of the eleven-member cabinet was made up of politicians who were more moderate than the Nazis. Vice chancellor Franz Von Papen and his political allies were to limit Hitler's power, but Hitler never settled for anything less than full control. He moved steadily toward dictatorship, and there was no place for freedom under his government, the Third Reich.

Through Frick's key position as minister of the interior, he controlled all national police authority. Goering controlled the Prussian police. An emergency decree signed by Hindenburg on February 4, 1933, gave the Nazis legal authority to prohibit assemblies, to outlaw newspapers and other publications, and to arrest people suspected of treason. The Nazis were able to put down much of their political opposition. Goering creating an auxiliary police force made up of thousands of stormtroopers—"ICE"—and ordered them to shoot when they encountered enemies.

These stormtroopers were nothing but the same racist bigots that we are dealing with now, America's own version of terrorists. Terrorists like Isis didn't just become terrorists when they blew something up. They have been waiting for the call to terrorize those who they've been led to believe are their enemies.

Hate groups in this country now feel a little more emboldened to raise their heads again since Trump's campaign and election. I believe that they will be doing more once they receive the call from the White House to come out full force, with a license to arrest and murder nonwhites.

On March 23, 1933, the Nazis dominated the Reichstag. They passed a law for the removal of distress from the people and state. Known as the Enabling Act, it gave the government full dictatorial power and, in effect, suspended basic civil and human rights for four years. Once the president signed it, Hitler had a firm legal basis on which to govern as he pleased. He had also destroyed the constitution through outwardly legal means.

By mid-July 1933, the government had outlawed freedom of the press, all labor unions, and all political parties except the Nazi Party. The Gestapo (secret state police) hunted down the enemies and opponents of the government. People were jailed or shot on suspicion alone.

The Nazis used the press, radio, and films to flood Germany with propaganda praising the New Order, Hitler's term for his reordering of German society. I wonder if this is the same as Fox News.

Jews were forced out of the civil service, universities and other schools, and professional and managerial positions. In 1935 German Jews were declared citizens of lesser rights. Hitler directed the stormtroopers, Nazi officials, and members of the army and the civil service in a campaign of mass slaughter of about six million Jews. Over two thirds of the Jews of Europe were murdered, and more than three million Soviet prisoners of war were starved and worked to death. Hitler's victims also included large numbers of Roma (sometimes called gypsies), Poles, Slavs, Jehovah's Witnesses, priests and ministers, mental patients, and communist and other political opponents.

I want you to keep in mind that Donald Trump and many of his hate supporters share beliefs of the Nazis. Their core beliefs are that Nazi garbage. If you are not white, you're not right.

Hitler blamed the Jews for Germany's problems, and he made anti-Semitism government policy. The Nazi government continued to deprive Jews of their rights and possessions. Jews could not sit on park benches or swim in public pools. The government seized Jewish businesses and personal property. This discrimination was an effort to force Jews to immigrate so Germany would be free of Jews.

When Hitler murdered and imprisoned the Jews, he saved the ones who felt that what was happening to the rest of the Jews didn't apply to them. After all, they were rich people of influence, owners of big companies, or entertainers. Hitler saved them for last, but they all had to go.

Can you believe that while other Jews were being murdered and oppressed there were Jews who dined and partied with Nazis? Church leaders and influential Jews went along with their lives and closed their eyes to what was going on around them. This reminds me of the influential people of color in this country who are either ignorant about what's really going on, or just don't believe that it will ever affect their lives.

Under the Trump administration, the rules of government are being challenged. The checks and balances of the three branches, put in place by the founding fathers, are not working as planned. We can see now that a political party that controls the Senate and the White House, can be a real threat to our democracy. The Democrats run the House, but in the Senate and White House, they don't really have a voice. Since Republicans are in charge, we constantly hear that the Democrats are stopping this or that. Democrats can pass a thousand bills, but if the Senate, under its powerful majority leader Mitch McConnell of Kentucky, chooses not to bring them to the floor for a vote, those bills don't mean anything. Just ask the grand reaper.

We have a Republican president who wants to be a dictator. We have a Republican-led Senate that is supposed to make sure the president follows the law and the Constitution. The founding fathers emphasized checks and balances as a means of assuring individual freedom and avoiding government tyranny. In this regard, Congress has surely failed. The Republicans are not checking this president. They are allowing him to do whatever he wants. They confirm his nominees, many of whom the world knows are not qualified for the position.

The judicial branch is being stacked with Republican judges, perfect for a wannabe dictator. All three branches are supposed to be separate, but how can that be working when we have members of the judicial and legislative branches more loyal to the president than to the US Constitution?

We have a president who is so hateful and racist that he is constantly trying to convince all the people in the country that all immigrants are criminals, including the ones who have lived here all their lives and never even had a parking ticket. He has attacked the Dreamers. Though they are model citizens, he said that they had to go too.

What has the poor and oppressed done to earn such hatred, other than not being white and the fear that black and brown people will take over America. Please stop with the paranoia. White people have the military and most of the money and power. But with all that, they are still afraid of people with no money, no real power, and no real weapons. They must be insecure.

Immigrants came to this beautiful country looking for opportunities and to make better lives for themselves and their families. If that means doing any job and accepting any pay, that's what they are willing to do with prayer and hope that things will get better. So why are people mad at them? The anger is misplaced. Immigrants are not making businesses hire them. And remember that most people came to this country seeking the same opportunities and praying for the same chances for their families.

Big business and the government are co-defendants. They

are the main problem when it comes to unemployment. They shortchange American people by looking for ways to hire people who will accept any amount of payment without any concern for the people in the country just looking for a fair wage to support their families. I have found that the business communities are so slick they will advertise that they are hiring just so they can say they tried to hire American workers first. Just ask Trump; he knows all about that scam. Now we have thousands of people graduating from trade schools and colleges. They are thousands of dollars in debt, and many can't find employment. Most business advertising asks that the applicant have at least two to four years of experience, not including internships. Basically, people are going into debt trying to get a good job. How can they receive experience if they can't get hired? What a scam.

Where Is Religion?

Where are the so-called religious people? You know, the ones that preach love everybody, care for the hungry and homeless, and welcome the stranger. I say so-called religious people because they are not standing on the principles of God as they claim to know him though they speak the words very well. It is very hard to find the real followers of Christ and Muhammad.

Where are the religious leaders? Where is the faith that they all preach about? I don't see you. And because of the internet, the youth in the world don't see you or their family members living the faith that is so often talked about. So how do you think they really see you?

Those kinds of religious leaders and followers were doing the same things during slavery and the Holocaust. They turned their heads while injustice was going on all around them. They remained silent when members of their faith and family and friends raped, beat, killed, and separated slaves from their families. They stood silent when Hitler was murdering the Jews. These are the same people who find all kinds of excuses to vote for Donald Trump. His message of hate does not disturb them.

Some religious services preach about the words "love," "kindness," and "respect" and how we should treat each other. But their hearts are far from it. If they can find any reason to support hate, prejudice, and racism, then they are just reading their religious books and not applying the words to their lives.

If you read your Bible, you will read that the Jerry Falwells of the world are the so-called religious people Jesus Christ described who were in the temples representing man's laws, not God's. It amazes me how these so-called religious leaders can see hate, oppression, ethnic cleansing, hunger, sickness, poverty, and corruption all over the world. They speak out against this. They raise money to help fight this. But here at home, they turn their heads to the same problems, including police brutality, mass incarceration (enslaving their own people for profit), mass homelessness, and hunger.

I see some churches handing out tents and food, but what's that all about? They have the power and influence to make a major difference in this country. They can make a difference in such issues as poverty, lack of opportunity, affordable housing, a better educational system, and a way for young people to earn money legally, allowing them to leave their crime-ridden neighborhoods and enjoy the good— and affordable—things their cities have to offer them. Keep your tents, your water, and your food. Start making a real difference. Start doing God's work. Stop turning your head to the injustice of the poor and oppressed. Speak to your representatives and make a difference.

I ask again, where is their religion? They remain silent when millions of Americans might lose their health coverage under the Trump administration. They remain silent while social programs are being taken from the poor by the Trump administration. They remain silent when the Trump administration allows big business to pollute the air and poison our water. They remain silent while Trump pushes hate and divides the country. They remain silent while Trump makes policies that separate children from their families and puts them in cages. Aren't they God's children too?

Why is the religious community not shouting, "Liar," and, "Blasphemy?" Trump has compared himself to Jesus. Jesus was compassionate. Jesus didn't have a filthy mouth. He didn't lie, he didn't molest and disrespect women. Jesus came to bring us together and to teach us how to love one another. Not to divide us, not to have us scared of and hating each other. Jesus wouldn't take children from their families and put them in cages. He definitely wouldn't play a part in traumatizing children. Jesus would have helped Puerto Rico. He wouldn't be trying to get rid of all social programs. Jesus cared about the plight of the poor. For those who say that Trump might be like Jesus, please tell us how you came to that conclusion.

SIX

PLEASE STOP TALKING

You don't know what's going on in our communities. You don't represent us. You are so out of touch with what is really going on with us. You have money and fame. Stay in your lane if you don't know what you're talking about.

People out here are really struggling. You don't see it just like you can't see the struggle a drug addict goes through trying to stay clean. There's a war being waged, and just like throughout history, there have always been your kind. You can never see anything wrong with how we are treated. "Don't they feed us and let us sleep in the barn? So what they call us all kinds of nasty names. That's just how white people talk."

Dr. Ben Carson, you should be ashamed of yourself. You are old enough to recognize a racist when you see one. You are the only black with a real position in the Trump administration, and you ain't even in the White House. To a person like Trump, you are just a token black.

Lil Wayne, the rapper, thinks racism is over, and he can't relate to black lives matter. Please shut up. You sound stupid.

Didn't you see the Nazis and KKK marching in the streets in 2017? That's racism. Do you see the police searching a tour bus of white entertainers? Do you see the mass incarceration of blacks and Latinos like we are the only ones breaking laws? That's racism.

Rapper Kanye West wants us to stop focusing on racism. He said that he didn't vote, but if he had, he would have voted for Trump. If our people don't focus on what's going on around us, we may find ourselves in a civil war for our freedom again. You are another embarrassment to our people. Racism is still alive and well. You and Mike Tyson think that because Trump treats you like you're somebody special. You are being played. It is to his benefit to treat you like that. We all know that he loves any chance to look important. To him, you and Mike Tyson are just some other blacks he can use.

Charles Barkley, Mr. Basketball, blames black people for the violence and the treatment they face at the hands of the police. Mr. Don't Know What's Going On Barkley, please do your research about what's really up with law enforcement in this country before you go back on the road, preaching that garbage about how the police are misunderstood. These same misunderstood police are terrorizing the communities in this country. They are not following the laws; they are making their own laws. They are in our communities raping, robbing, and assaulting anybody they feel like. Even when they're on video violating someone's rights, you can always make some kind of excuse for their behavior. They are a legalized gang with licenses to kill, assault, sell drugs, rape, and rob. Our communities are defenseless. Law enforcement has a free hand to do what they want, and Congress and the courts support them. The White House supports them, and racist Jeff Sessions and you and your kind supports them. Every time the courts dismiss the evidence that's on video, they send the message that police can kill all of us, and there won't be any consequences.

Shaquille O'Neal, the basketball player, Shaq, said he's never worried when he is stopped by a cop because he shows respect to the officers. Man, you are Shaq, and that respect stuff works for you. We can be nice and let the officer know that he's in charge, and still have our car searched, be arrested for nothing, and maybe killed.

Willie Dove, a black Donald Trump supporter, said, "I don't think anything he says is racist." He must not know what racism looks like. Even white people say that the president is a bigot and racist. Every time I see you on TV, I am ashamed that you are a black man aiding this administration in its efforts to deport Latinos, who are just trying to make better lives for their children, and disenfranchise and incarcerate black people for refusing to be poor. Martin Luther King Jr. had to push back on a lot of your kind.

Pastor Darrell Scott, a Cleveland pastor, says that many African Americans support Donald Trump privately. What does he mean by "many"? Is he talking about the millions who are unemployed or the ones who are working? Please get your facts right before you speak for black people. The Obama administration left Trump with a country that was coming out of a financial crisis and headed in the right direction. No big world conflicts and millions with health care who never had it before. He had started correcting this country's race-based mass incarceration of blacks and Latinos. The economy was on the move. There was less unemployment, and it was predicted that there would be a large decrease in unemployment, and the economy would get a lot better. So stop lying. Trump did not create the millions of new jobs; the millions were created by the

Obama administration. The truth is Trump created some jobs, but not millions.

Jack Brewer, former NFL player, calls Trump the first black president. You are the worst of the worst black boot-lickers. The man is a race hater. What does he have to do, come with the KKK to your door and personally drag you out? Just another black helping master. You are the kind who would do and say anything to help his cause.

In closing, Donald Trump is a master at manipulation. He said the Democrats were going to try to steal the election from the Republicans. Smart move. The Obama administration could not expose the information that they had discovered because it would appear they were trying to steal the election from him. Real smart. Trump said they would say things about him and his campaign, but they shouldn't believe them. It was all fake news. Another smart move.

Trump convinced America that he was the only one telling the truth was him. He set the fire, hollered fire, and got credit for alerting everyone that there was a fire. Masterful.

To his supporters, why is it that you don't find the need to challenge your president? When he is challenged on any issue, his defense is always that it's fake news and that the Democrats are out to get him. His accusers present all kinds of evidence, but you still go for his same lines—fake news and Democrats are out to get him. If that is all you need from him, you are in a cult! I also want him and his supporters to know that white people received more government assistance than blacks and browns. Do your research before you lose your benefits (Ryan Sit, "Trump Thinks Only Black People Are on Welfare, but Really, White Americans Receive Most Benefits, *Newsweek*, 1/12/18). In fact, whites are the biggest beneficiaries when it comes to government safety-net programs like the Temporary Assistance for Needy Families, commonly referred to as welfare.

Thanks for taking the time to read my book. I hope it gave you some facts that you didn't know before. I ask that you do your own research. Facts do matter.

FOREWORD

ABOUT THE AUTHOR

Curtis Dupree wrote this book to reveal the truth about what's happening to poor people in the United States of America.